When There is H.O.P.E

Healing

Overcomes

Painful

Events

DEVOTIONAL

By
Bridgette M. Alfred

When There is H.O.P.E Devotional

©2021 by Bridgette M. Alfred

All rights reserved. No portion of this publication may be reproduced, stored in a retrieval system, or transmitted in any form or by any means–electronic, mechanical, photocopying, recording, scanning, or other–except for brief quotations in critical reviews or articles, without the prior written permission of the publisher.

Published in Hampton, VA, by Fruition Publishing Concierge Services. Fruition Publishing Concierge Services is a division of Alesha Brown, LLC.

Fruition Publishing Concierge Services can bring authors to your live event. For more information or to book an event, visit Fruition Publishing Concierge Services at

www.FruitionPublishing.com

ISBN: 978-1-954486-13-3 Paperback

ISBN: 978-1-954486-14-0 eBook

Library of Congress Control Number: 2021912752

Unless otherwise noted, all scriptures are from The Holy Bible, New International Version. (1984). Grand Rapids: Zondervan Publishing House.

ACKNOWLEDGMENTS

All praise and honor go to My ABBA Father! Without Him, this devotional book of prayers would not have been possible. With His inspiration, I was able to pour out my heart, mind, and soul.

My sincere gratitude for the professionalism of Alesha Brown and Fruition Publishing Concierge Services.

Table of Contents

The God of Hope 3
God Is In The Restoration Business 5
What Is Hope? 7
Hope, Faith, and Love 9
An Anchor For The Soul 11
Believing Is Receiving 13
The Symbol of Faith 15
God is Love 17
Chasing The Heart of God 19
A Loving Heart 21
Character of Heart 23
Quitting Is Not An Option 25
There Is Nothing New 27
God Uses The Ordinary 29
Father Knows Best 31
Sovereign God 33
A Fresh Beginning 35
Focus On God 37
This World Needs Love 39
Weakness vs. Strength 41
Have The God Kind of Faith 43
Lead By Example 45
Your Promises Are Yes and Amen 47
Choices of Life 49
God's Word Is Truth 51
Follow the Leader 53
Mountain Moving Faith 55
Choices Have Consequences 57

Attitude Determines Altitude	59
God Can Use a Few Good Warriors	61
A Christian Life	63
Make Godly Decisions	65
We Are Family	67
Show The Love Of God	69
World Changers	71
I Got A Testimony	73
God Loves Prodigals	75
Do You Believe in Miracles?	77
Our Hope Is In God	79
God Hears Our Prayers	81
In God I Trust	83
The Cross	85
My Heart Longs	87
Children Are a Blessing	89
Show Compassion	91
Victory Is Mine	93
Do You Know The Truth?	95
Depend On Jesus	97
Restored World	99
Random Acts of Kindness	101
Love	103
The Great Commandment	105
God Is Omnipresent	107
Can You Hear Me Now?	109
Words of Encouragement	111
Share Love	113
Be A Blessing	115
God Created You For A Purpose	117
God Equipped Me For My Assignment	119

All My Children	121
Seeking God	123
Step By Step, Day By Day	125
Forgiveness Heals	127
God Sees Our Tears	129
Seek Good Counsel	131
God's Gift Of Children	133
History Or Destiny?	135
Choose The Road to Excellence	137
Helpers Of One Another	139
Unconditional Love	141
Two Become One	143
Harmonious Marriage	145
Peace Of Mind	147
Two Ears, One Mouth	149
Compromise As a Solution	151
Fully Committed	153
No Hide-And-Seek With God	155
God Is My Help	157
A Brighter Future	159
Wisdom	161
Help In Times Of Trouble	163
God's Thoughts	165
The Word Doesn't Fail	167
Labor Of Love	169
Live A Life Of Love	171
Christ Is My Anchor	173
No Expiration Date	175
New Mercies Every Day	177
Wait On The Lord	179
A Word Of Promise	181

The Peace Maker	183
Overflow With Hope	185
The Love Of God Has No Limits	187
Faith Is Essential	189
Love One Another	191
The Lord's Mercies	193
Stay On Guard	195
Hope Is In The Bible	197
Faith Walk	199
Everlasting Love	201
Present and Future	203
The Right Answer	205
God Is My Rock	207
Deliverance Is Near	209
The Glory	211
Don't Be Discouraged	213
The Good News	215
Safety From Harm	217
The Inheritance	219
All My Help	221
Feed Your Soul	223
More Than A Conqueror	225
Pursue The Prince Of Peace	227
Praises	229
The Comforter	231
The Eyes Of The Lord	233
Dreams Do Come True!	235
Heavenly Home	237
The Divine High Priest	239
Walk In Truth	241
The Kingdom Of Heaven	243

Thankful In Prayer	245
The High Calling	247
A Living Hope	249
Hope In The Future	251
The Priceless Gift	253
The Unforgettable God	255
The Good Reward	257
Equip For Battle	259
The Father's Gift	261
Faithful Promise	263
Keep His Ways	265
Uncertain Riches	267
Hope Is ... For You	269
Believe In God's Promise	271
Do You Need Hope?	273
Where Is Your Trust?	275
Needs vs Wants	277
God Is The Hope And Glory	279
Confess Hope	281
God's Mercy	283
Where Does Your Help Come From?	285
Salvation Prayer	287
Prayer To Mend Which Is Broken	289
About the Author	291

Introduction

We all need Hope because life can be hard. Sometimes, we must endure a bad day. Other times, we face heartache. No amount of tears can bring it to an end.

Most of us face difficult times more often than we would like. Yet, as difficult as life can be, Hope guides us and gets us through the storms of life. Take away Hope and even the small things crush us.

As we look at the big picture in our world, we see hopeless situations. The news regularly blasts us with stories of the harmful and even evil situations people endure. Abuse, divorce, murder, war, famine, rape, and natural disasters torment our lives and shred our broken world. Beyond the unexpected disasters that make the news, we're wounded by the daily actions of others who never get headlines but hurt us deeply.

Hope is a feeling of expectation and desire for a certain thing to happen. Hope is an optimistic attitude of mind that is based on an expectation of positive outcomes, related events, and circumstances in one's life or the world at large. Hope is a strong certainty that what God has promised in the Bible is true, has occurred, and or will be in accordance with His sure Word.

God is called "the God of Hope," which means He is the source of all *real* Hope. If we are going to have Hope, it must come from Him for He alone has the power to give it. If this is true, you might wonder how God can allow bad things to happen to good people. *Is this how God intended us to live? Is this the kind of life He created us for?* Thankfully, the answer is no.

The Bible tells us the true story of how God created us and our world, how we fell away from His original design, and what He did to heal our brokenness. It offers Hope because we discover that God is in the business of restoring us to His beautiful original intentions.

The Hope of eternal life endures even while the believer struggles with life's challenges. The worldly hope is no hope at all, but Hope in Christ is a firm and secure anchor of the soul. **Hebrews 6:19** describes the Hope we have in Christ:

We have this Hope as a sure and steadfast anchor of the soul, which enters the Inner Place behind the veil.

The soul, according to the biblical definition, is the mind, the will, and the emotions. An anchor serves to hold a boat firmly. Therefore, when the winds of life are blowing, circumstances are surrounding your purpose and life isn't going how you planned, Hope in Jesus is an anchor to keep your mind, your will, and your emotions steady.

There is, however, a very interesting thing about having one's mind, will, and emotions anchored in the Hope that is Christ. If you believe you have no anchor - even though you do - you will respond as if the wind and waves of life are overtaking you and that you are perishing. When you could have peace, you'll be panicking, fretting, and feeling hopeless. Even though God has said that you have a firm and secure Hope, you will respond like you have no anchor.

There are some things that God has given that are undeniably yours, but you will only experience joy and peace knowing they are yours by believing. You have a Hope, steady and secure.

The **There is H.O.P.E Devotional** is written to give you a spiritual toolbox for your daily Christian journey. This devotional was inspired by my first fiction novel, "When There Is H.O.P.E. (Healing Over Past Events).

The God of Hope

Psalm 42:5: *Why, my soul, are you downcast? Why so disturbed within me? Put your hope in God, for I will yet praise him, my Savior, and my God.*

Jeremiah 14:22: *Do any of the worthless idols of the nations bring rain? Do the skies themselves send down showers? No, it is you, Lord our God. Therefore our hope is in you, for you are the one who does all this.*

Romans 15:13: *May the God of hope fill you with all joy and peace as you trust in him, so that you may overflow with hope by the power of the Holy Spirit.*

We all need Hope because life can be hard. Most of us face difficult times more often than we would like. Yet, as difficult as life can be, Hope guides us and gets us through the storms of life.

God is called "the God of Hope," which means He is the source of all real hope. If we are going to have Hope, it must come from Him for He alone has the power to give it.

ABBA Father, I thank You for being my God of Hope and loving me just as I am. Father, you are present even when I do not realize it or sense that you are there. I take time today to dwell in stillness that I might know the promise and presence of you. Thank you for giving me a desire to become more and to trust you and your will for my life. Amen.

God Is In The Restoration Business

Psalm 119:74: *May those who fear you rejoice when they see me, for I have put my hope in your word.*

Psalm 130:5: *I wait for the Lord, my whole being waits, and in his word I put my hope.*

Romans 15:4: *For everything that was written in the past was written to teach us, so that through the endurance taught in the Scriptures and the encouragement they provide we might have hope.*

The news regularly blasts us with stories of the harmful and even evil situations people endure. Beyond the unexpected disasters that make the news, we are wounded by the daily actions of others who never get headlines but hurt us deeply. We begin to wonder how God can allow bad things to happen to good people.

The Bible tells us the true story of how God created us and our world, how we fell away from His original design, and what He did to heal our brokenness. It offers hope because we discover that God is in the business of restoring us to His beautiful original intentions.

ABBA Father, I put away anything that substitutes for your presence and join all that I am, my deepest parts to Jesus. Father thank you for providing your Son to take my place, bearing the burden of my sins.

Open my eyes today to all the ways you still want to provide for me. Help me to recognize your provisions and to grow in understanding that you are ABBA Father who is always good.

I trust you to care for me no matter what I need. Help me to stay focus on what you have promised in the Bible. Amen.

What Is Hope?

Jeremiah 29:11-12: *For I know the plans I have for you, declares the Lord, plans to prosper you and not to harm you, plans to give you hope and a future. Then you will call on me and come and pray to me, and I will listen to you.*

Romans 8:25-26: *But if we hope for what we do not yet have, we wait for it patiently. In the same way, the Spirit helps us in our weakness. We do not know what we ought to pray for, but the Spirit himself intercedes for us through wordless groans.*

Hebrews 6:10-11: *God is not unjust; he will not forget your work and the love you have shown him as you have helped his people and continue to help them. We want each of you to show this same diligence to the very end, so that what you hope for may be fully realized.*

Hope is a feeling of expectation and desire for a certain thing to happen. Hope is an optimistic attitude of mind that is based on an expectation of positive outcomes, related events, and circumstances in one's life or the world at large. Hope is a strong certainty that what God has promised in the Bible is true, has occurred, and or will be in accordance with God's sure Word.

DEVOTIONAL

ABBA Father, help me today to put all my Hope in you. I seek today not to live by the limitations of my circumstances, problems, thoughts, and ways. I live by faith beyond them.

Father, when I get too fearful about things that I cannot control in any way, please remind me that you are still in control. Help me to trust in your certainty and Hope. Amen.

Hope, Faith, and Love

1 Corinthians 13:13: *So now faith, hope, and love abide, these three; but the greatest of these is love.*

Philippians 4:8-9: *Finally, brothers and sisters, whatever is true, whatever is noble, whatever is right, whatever is pure, whatever is lovely, whatever is admirable—if anything is excellent or praiseworthy—think about such things. Whatever you have learned or received or heard from me or seen in me—put it into practice. And the God of peace will be with you.*

1 John 4:7-9: *Dear friends, let us love one another, for love comes from God. Everyone who loves has been born of God and knows God. Whoever does not love does not know God, because God is love. This is how God showed his love among us: He sent his one and only Son into the world that we might live through him.*

There are three specific symbolisms for the Christian journey through life: The anchor represents a grounding (Hope) securely connected to the cross (Faith). The heart symbol (Love) represents love and affection for others.

The symbols of Hope, Faith, and Love represent the three theological virtues that God puts into a believer's soul. We must live our lives according to these virtues to be worthy of eternal life.

ABBA Father, I seek today not to increase what I have, but to increase my thanks for what I have. I give thanks in all things. The greater my thanksgiving, the greater will be my life.

From this moment on, I purpose to walk in love, to seek peace, to live in agreement, and to conduct myself toward others in a manner that is pleasing to you. I know that I have right standing with you and your ears are attentive to my prayers.

I thank you for Hope, Faith, and Love to successfully walk my Christian journey. Amen.

An Anchor For The Soul

1 Timothy 1:1-2: *Paul, an apostle of Christ Jesus by the command of God our Savior and of Christ Jesus our hope, To Timothy my true son in the faith: Grace, mercy and peace from God the Father and Christ Jesus our Lord.*

Hebrews 6:19-20: *We have this hope as an anchor for the soul, firm and secure. It enters the inner sanctuary behind the curtain, where our forerunner, Jesus, has entered on our behalf. He has become a high priest forever, in the order of Melchizedek.*

1 Peter 1:3-5: *Praise be to the God and Father of our Lord Jesus Christ! In his great mercy he has given us new birth into a living hope through the resurrection of Jesus Christ from the dead, and into an inheritance that can never perish, spoil, or fade. This inheritance is kept in heaven for you, who through faith are shielded by God's power until the coming of the salvation that is ready to be revealed in the last time.*

The worldly hope is no hope at all but Hope in Christ is a firm and secure anchor of the soul. The soul is the mind, the will, and the emotions. An anchor serves to hold a boat firmly. Therefore, when the winds of life are blowing, circumstances are surrounding your purpose, and life is not going how you planned, Hope in Jesus is an anchor to keep your mind, your will, and your emotions steady.

Lord Jesus, today I take the smallest of actions, but in a new direction, the first step toward the life of victory. I have been called to live a new journey.

Jesus, you are the light that shines on all those living in darkness and the shadow of death. Shine your light on me now and guide my feet into the path of peace.

Thank you that no matter what circumstances are surrounding me, I can always depend on you being my anchor. Amen.

Believing Is Receiving

Isaiah 43:10-11 (MEV): *You are My witnesses, says the Lord, and My servant whom I have chosen that you may know and believe Me, and understand that I am He. Before Me there was no God formed, nor shall there be after Me. I, even I, am the Lord, and besides Me there is no savior.*

1 Thessalonians 2:13 (MEV): *For this reason we thank God without ceasing because, when you received the word of God, which you heard from us, you received it not as the word of men, but as it truly is, the word of God, which effectively works also in you who believe.*

Hebrews 10:23 (MEV): *Let us hold unswervingly to the hope we profess, for He who promised is faithful.*

There is a remarkably interesting thing about having one's mind, will, and emotions anchored in the Hope that is Christ. If you believe you have no anchor, you will respond as if life is over taking you. When you could have peace, you will be panicking and feeling hopeless. Even though God has said that you have a firm and secure Hope, you will respond like you have no anchor.

There are some things that God has given that are undeniably yours, but you will only experience the joy and peace knowing they are yours by believing. You have a Hope that is steady and secure.

ABBA Father, today I seek You on how to only believe in the Hope that is in you. I move away from the earthbound everything in my life that is tied to the world, to the flesh, and to sin. I move into the realm of the Heavenly. I start flying.

Father, help me to see the good in every situation, not giving up when the storms come, but rejoicing always in the coming sunshine. Amen.

The Symbol of Faith

1 Corinthians 1:17-18: *For Christ did not send me to baptize, but to preach the Gospel—not with wisdom and eloquence, lest the cross of Christ be emptied of its power. For the message of the cross is foolishness to those who are perishing, but to us who are being saved it is the power of God.*

Philippians 2:8-11: *And being found in appearance as a man, he humbled himself by becoming obedient to death—even death on a cross! Therefore God exalted him to the highest place and gave him the name that is above every name, that at the name of Jesus every knee should bow, in heaven and on earth and under the earth, and every tongue acknowledge that Jesus Christ is Lord, to the glory of God the Father.*

1 Peter 2:24: *"He himself bore our sins" in his body on the cross, so that we might die to sins and live for righteousness; "by his wounds you have been healed."*

The cross, representing faith, symbolizes the believer's deep trust in all that God has revealed is true. The cross of faith is important because believers are expected to share with others their faith in God's truth. No matter how rough life gets, the believer is always attached to the source of faith. The Gospel tells us that the Lord Jesus spoke of the significance of the cross before His death to His disciples (Matthew 10:38 and Luke 14:27).

Lord Jesus, I take all the unfulfilled longings, needs, and desires of my life and turn them away from the worldly and to the Heavenly. A seed cannot bear fruit unless it first falls into the ground and dies.

I confess that I am with Christ: nevertheless, I live; yet not I, but Christ lives in me. And the life that I now live in the flesh I live by the faith of the Son of God, who loved me and gave Himself for me. I can never thank you enough for all you did for me on the cross. Amen.

God is Love

Joshua 22:5 (MEV): *Only carefully obey the commandment and the law that Moses the servant of the Lord commanded you: to love the Lord your God, to walk in all His ways, to obey His commandments, to cling to Him, and to serve Him with all your heart and soul.*

Psalm 130:7 (MEV): *Israel, put your hope in the Lord, for with the Lord is unfailing love and with him is full redemption.*

Matthew 22:37-39 (MEV): *Jesus said to him, 'You shall love the Lord your God with all your heart, and with all your soul, and with all your mind.' This is the first and great commandment. And the second is like it: 'You shall love your neighbor as yourself.'*

The heart is the inner self that thinks, feels, and makes decisions. The heart is that which is central to a person. The heart symbol represents love and affection for others.

Believers strive to love God and to love others as God loves them. Love symbolizes the desire to love everyone, including one's enemies, neighbors, and the poor. Love cannot be achieved without faith and Hope because the three are interlocked together.

ABBA Father, I thank you for loving me unconditionally. I seek this day to know the love you have for me. It is always new and never-ending from you.

Father, thank you for blessing my life with beauty. I am captivated by your work and hope to become even more aware of all that you have provided for me to enjoy. I must follow you and love others the same way. Amen.

Chasing The Heart of God

Psalm 73:26 (MEV): *My flesh and my heart fails, but God is the strength of my heart and my portion forever.*

Romans 5:5 (MEV): *And hope does not disappoint, because the love of God is shed abroad in our hearts by the Holy Spirit who has been given to us.*

Ezekiel 36:26 (MEV): *Also, I will give you a new heart, and a new spirit I will put within you. And I will take away the stony heart out of your flesh, and I will give you a heart of flesh.*

Nearly all the references to the heart in the Bible refer to the same aspect of human personality. The source of life is rendered a heart (Ephesians 6:6), "doing the will of God from the heart."

In the Bible, all emotions are experienced by the heart: love and hate (Psalm 105:25 and 1 Peter 1:22), joy and sorrow (Ecclesiastes 2:10 and John 16:6), peace and bitterness (Ezekiel 27:31 and Colossians 3:15), and fear (Genesis 42:28).

DEVOTIONAL

ABBA Father, I live this day as a Heavenly light. I live as a living sacrifice, a gift for Your purposes. I will shine like the stars. I thank You for filling me with the knowledge of Your Will in all wisdom and spiritual understanding that I may walk worthy of You. Father help me to be fruitful in every good work and increase in the knowledge of You. Help me to be Your child who is chasing after Your heart. Amen.

A Loving Heart

John 13:34 (MEV): *A new commandment I give to you, that you love one another, even as I have loved you, that you also love one another.*

1 Thessalonians 1:2-3 (MEV): *We give thanks to God always for you all, mentioning you in our prayers, remembering without ceasing your work of faith, labor of love, and patient hope in our Lord Jesus Christ in the sight of God and our Father.*

1 Peter 4:7-9 (MEV): *The end of all things is near. Therefore be solemn and sober so you can pray. Above all things, have unfailing love for one another, because love covers a multitude of sins. Show hospitality to one another without complaining.*

The thinking processes are said to be carried out by the heart. This intellectual activity corresponds to what would be called the mind in English. Thus, the heart may think (Esther 6:6), understand (Job 38:36), imagine (Jeremiah 9:14), remember (Deuteronomy 4:9), be wise (Proverbs 2:10), and speak to itself (Deuteronomy 7:17).

Decision-making is also carried out by the heart. Purpose (Acts 11:23), intention (Hebrews 4:12), and will (Ephesians 6:6) are all activities of the heart.

ABBA Father, I ponder the love that you have for me that has already endured for an eternity and will not cease or fail me now. I live accordingly.

Father, I will do unto others as I would have them do unto me. I eagerly pursue and seek to acquire this agape love. I purpose to make it my aim, my great quest in life. Help me to pour out love from my heart to everyone I encounter today. Amen.

Character of Heart

Psalm 51:10 (MEV): *Create in me a clean heart, O God, and renew a right spirit within me.*

Proverbs 3:5-6 (MEV): *Trust in the Lord with all your heart and lean not on your own understanding; in all your ways acknowledge Him, and He will direct your paths.*

Hebrews 10:22-23 (MEV): *… let us draw near with a true heart in full assurance of faith, having our hearts sprinkled to cleanse them from an evil conscience, and our bodies washed with pure water. Let us firmly hold the profession of our faith without wavering, for He who promised is faithful.*

The heart reveals everyone's true character or personality: purity or evil (Jeremiah 3:17 and Matthew 5:8), sincerity or hardness (Exodus 4:21 and Colossians 3:22), and rebelliousness (Jeremiah 5:23). God knows the heart of each person (1 Samuel 16:7).

Since we speak and act from our hearts, we are to guard them well (Proverbs 4:23 and Matthew 15:18-19). The most important commitment of anyone is to love God with the whole heart (Matthew 22:37). With the heart, a person believes in Christ and so experience both love from God and the presence of Christ in the heart (Romans 5:5; 10:9-10 and Ephesians 3:17).

ABBA Father, I pray today that you show me the true character of my heart. What are my possessions? I let go and free up my heart of its earthly possessions. I fill up my heart with the Spiritual and Heavenly.

Father, prepare me for the battles that will come. Help me to hold up the cross of your Son as the banner over my life. Let the victories I enjoy be credited to you so that all may rally to your cause. Amen.

Quitting Is Not An Option

Isaiah 40:31 (MEV): *But those who wait upon the Lord shall renew their strength; they shall mount up with wings as eagles, they shall run and not be weary, and they shall walk and not faint.*

Romans 15:4-6: *For everything that was written in the past was written to teach us, so that through the endurance taught in the Scriptures and the encouragement they provide we might have hope. May the God who gives endurance and encouragement give you the same attitude of mind toward each other that Christ Jesus had, so that with one mind and one voice you may glorify the God and Father of our Lord Jesus Christ.*

1 Thessalonians 1:2-3: *We always thank God for all of you and continually mention you in our prayers. We remember before our God and Father your work produced by faith, your labor prompted by love, and your endurance inspired by hope in our Lord Jesus Christ.*

Each season of our lives, we may have someone to encourage or motivate us. But our character also helps us to endure the many significant life-changing events throughout our lives.

Many times, we may be knocked down, but we do not have to stay down. We might lose a few battles, but we only lose the war if we wave a white flag and surrender. With Jesus, we can persevere with a supernatural inner strength to press on and not quit from life's adversities.

Lord Jesus, today I surrender my strong will and independent mindset to your will. Today, I come as I am, with no covering or pretense, confessing what I must confess. Then I receive my blessing.

Jesus, I thank you for making a comeback in my life over and over again. Every time I manage to step away from you, I discover that it is not long before I miss having you close to me again. Thank you for always staying true to me. Amen.

There Is Nothing New

Colossian 1:4-6 (MEV): *For we heard of your faith in Christ Jesus and your love for all the saints, because of the hope, which is laid up for you in heaven, of which you have already heard in the word of the truth of the Gospel.*

2 Thessalonians 2:14-15 (MEV): *To this He called you by our Gospel, to obtain the glory of our Lord Jesus Christ. Therefore, brothers, stand firm and hold the traditions which you have been taught, whether by word or by our letter.*

2 Timothy 3:16-17 (MEV): *All Scripture is inspired by God and is profitable for teaching, for reproof, for correction, and for instruction in righteousness, that the man of God may be complete, thoroughly equipped for every good work.*

During life's journey, we have our valley lows and mountain highs. How we approach them makes all the difference.

Due to human nature, we often attempt to solve our problems but only make them worst. Studying the Bible and learning about the lives of the characters in the Bible can be an encouraging endeavor for several reasons.

First, many of the Bible characters are famous, and they have found permanent places in the Western culture. The Bible's characters also show positive virtues that can be imitated. "What has been is the same as what will be, and what has been done is the same as what will be done; there is nothing new under the sun." (Ecclesiastes 1:9)

Dear Lord, today I need to have a hunger for studying the Bible more. I let Jesus's love come through my life. I lift your name, Jesus. You are the One that has created me by your great power. You are the great God of the universe and yet you chose to give me a Bible full of blessed promises to live by.

Thank You for writing down your covenant in the Holy Scriptures. Thank you for loving me so much that you gave to me the precious covenant of the cross. I worship and adore you, my ABBA. Amen.

God Uses The Ordinary

Acts 4:13: *When they saw the courage of Peter and John and realized that they were unschooled, ordinary men, they were astonished, and they took note that these men had been with Jesus.*

2 Corinthians 4:7 (NET): *But we have this treasure in clay jars, so that the extraordinary power belongs to God and does not come from us.*

James 5:17 (CEB): *Elijah was a person just like us. When he earnestly prayed that it wouldn't rain, no rain fell for three and a half years.*

There are plenty of evil villains in the Bible. Even the Bible's heroes are shown with their flaws. The very realism with which the Bible presents its heroes and villains is strength.

The Bible shows God accomplishing many great things using people who were not models of virtue. Rather, God used ordinary people. In today's complex and challenging world, that lesson can be comforting and encouraging.

ABBA Father, today I focus only on one course, one path, one journey, one destination, and one direction which is up. I aim to go higher with every step. I submit to Godly wisdom that I might learn to control my tongue.

I renounce, reject, and repent of every word that has ever proceeded out of my mouth against you, Father, and your kingdom. I cancel its power and dedicate my mouth to speak excellent and right things. My mouth shall utter truth. I am willing to be used by you to accomplish extraordinary things. Amen.

Father Knows Best

Isaiah 55:8-9 (MEV): *For My thoughts are not your thoughts, nor are your ways My ways, says the Lord. For as the heavens are higher than the earth, so are My ways higher than your ways, and My thoughts than your thoughts.*

Jeremiah 29:11 (MEV): *For I know the plans that I have for you, says the Lord, plans for peace and not for evil, to give you a future and a hope.*

Matthew 6:31-33 (CEV): *Don't worry and ask yourselves, "Will we have anything to eat? Will we have anything to drink? Will we have any clothes to wear?" Only people who don't know God are always worrying about such things. Your Father in heaven knows that you need all of these. But more than anything else, put God's work first and do what he wants. Then the other things will be yours as well.*

At times, we may experience life events that uproot our lives from the culture, customs, and family that we are familiar with. These events can sometimes cause emotional, spiritual, and physical pain in our lives. But we are all unique and God has distinct plans for each one of us. We must trust and have hope in His plans and that they are far better than we can ever imagine.

ABBA Father, I thank you for your distinct plans for my life. Help me to answer with a resounding "Yes," when you call, and then bless me with the ability to do the task at hand. I must trust in the fact that you know what is best for me. Amen.

Sovereign God

Psalm 103:19 (TPT): *God's heavenly throne is eternal, secure, and strong, and his sovereignty rules the entire universe.*

Daniel 4:3 (LEB): *How great are his signs and wonders, how strong is his kingdom, an everlasting kingdom; and his sovereignty is from generation to generation.*

1 Timothy 6:13-15 (NRSV): *In the presence of God, who gives life to all things, and of Christ Jesus, who in his testimony before Pontius Pilate made the good confession, I charge you to keep the commandment without spot or blame until the manifestation of our Lord Jesus Christ, which he will bring about at the right time—he who is the blessed and only Sovereign, the King of kings and Lord of lords.*

The Book of Esther is called the Book of the Unmentioned God. Esther speaks of all the times the presence of God is not felt. His voice is not heard. His hand is not seen. There is no sign of His love or purpose. There are times He seems far away or not there at all.

You realize that when God seems hopelessly far away from you, He is still right there beside you, working every detail in your life for His purposes and your redemption. Trust God for in the end, His light will break the darkness, His goodness will prevail, and you will know that you were never alone.

DEVOTIONAL

ABBA Father, I praise you for being a Sovereign God. I give thanks today for all my blessings and all my blessings in disguise. Those of the past and the still disguised blessings of the present. Because I am the righteousness of Jesus, I set the course of my life for obedience, abundance, wisdom, health, and joy.

Thank you for my ultimate victory over my trials. Set a guard over my mouth and then the words of my mouth and my deeds shall show forth your righteousness and your salvation all my days. Amen.

A Fresh Beginning

Proverbs 23:17-18 (MEV): *Do not let your heart envy sinners, but always be zealous for the fear of the Lord. There is surely a future hope for you, and your hope will not be cut off.*

Isaiah 42:9 (MEV): *See, the former things have come to pass, and new things I declare; before they spring forth I tell you of them.*

Jeremiah 29:11 (MEV): *For I know the plans that I have for you, says the Lord, plans for peace and not for evil, to give you a future and a hope.*

There are tragic times in life when dreadful things happen to good people. At times, those we look to for help, harm us instead. Only God's healing, mercy, and grace can restore our sense of self-worth and provide a fresh beginning.

ABBA Father, I take every guilt, shame, sin, failure, regret, and mistake in my life and put Jesus' name on each one, then give to Him that which is His. Father, you are alive and working in me so I can boldly say my words are words of faith, power, love, and life. They produce good things in my life and the lives of others.

I choose your words for my lips and your will for my life. I thank you that in every stage of my life, you are faithful to keep your promises. Amen.

Focus On God

Psalm 91:14-15 (ISV): *Because he has focused his love on me, I will deliver him. I will protect him because he knows my name. When he calls out to me, I will answer him. I will be with him in his distress. I will deliver him, and I will honor him.*

Lamentations 3:25-26 (NIV): *The Lord is good to those whose hope is in Him, to the one who seeks Him; it is good to wait quietly for the salvation of the Lord.*

Philippians 3:13-14 (TPT): *I don't depend on my own strength to accomplish this; however I do have one compelling focus: I forget all of the past as I fasten my heart to the future instead. I run straight for the divine invitation of reaching the heavenly goal and gaining the victory-prize through the anointing of Jesus.*

In this present time, people are overly impressed by the outward appearance. Sometimes it seems that God alone cares about what He sees in the heart. We must learn to keep our focus on God and not lean to our own understanding.

Embrace that unconditional love and Hope that is found in God. God blesses each of us in different ways. We need to praise Him for the gifts He gives us and not mourn for what we do not have.

ABBA Father, what problem, evil, or wrong am I dealing with? I do not dwell on it. I do not react. I dwell on its opposite. I overcome the dark with the light. I humble myself under your mighty hand that, in due time, you may exalt me.

I cast the whole of my cares - all my anxieties, worries, concerns once and for all on you. You care for me affectionately and care about me watchfully. You sustain me and today I will keep my focus on you. Amen.

This World Needs Love

Proverbs 3:3-4: *Let love and faithfulness never leave you; bind them around your neck, write them on the tablet of your heart. Then you will win favor and a good name in the sight of God and man.*

1 Corinthians 13:4-8 (MEV): *Love suffers long and is kind; love envies not; love flaunts not itself and is not puffed up, does not behave itself improperly, seeks not its own, is not easily provoked, thinks no evil; rejoices not in iniquity, but rejoices in the truth; bears all things, believes all things, hopes all things, and endures all things. Love never fails.*

1 John 4:16 (MEV): *And we have come to know and to believe the love that God has for us. God is love. Whoever lives in love lives in God, and God in him.*

Throughout the Bible, we are shown the steadfast love of God for His people. There is no doubt that God is love. Love is not just a feeling or emotion. We have the choice to love someone. That love should be genuine and unconditional like our Heavenly Father loves us.

Our daily walk must reflect a deep compassion, strong loyalty, and commitment to God and His Will. Let us be a sensitive and compassionate spokesperson for righteousness.

ABBA Father, daily I will live the prophetic message of love for you and the world. I share your love with someone who needs to be saved.

Father, I delight myself in you and you perfect that which concerns me. Thank you, Father, that I am carefree and walk in that peace that passes understanding. Amen.

Weakness vs. Strength

2 Samuel 22:3 (MEV): *He said: The Lord is my rock and my fortress and my deliverer; the God of my strength, in whom I will trust; my shield and the horn of my salvation, my fortress and my sanctuary; my Savior, You save me from violence.*

Psalm 18:1-2 (MEV): *I love You, O Lord, my strength. The Lord is my pillar, and my fortress, and my deliverer; my God, my rock, in whom I take refuge; my shield, and the horn of my salvation, my high tower.*

Isaiah 40:28-31 (MEV): *Have you not known? Have you not heard that the everlasting God, the Lord, the Creator of the ends of the earth, does not faint, nor is He weary? His understanding is inscrutable. He gives power to the faint, and to those who have no might He increases strength. Even the youths shall faint and be weary, and the young men shall utterly fall, but those who wait upon the Lord shall renew their strength; they shall mount up with wings as eagles, they shall run and not be weary, and they shall walk and not faint.*

In life, we need grace to live with things we cannot change and to have faith in God who works in all things for our good. Out of our weakness, we are made strong by the power of the Lord.

All of us have great potential but we can fall short because of sin and disobedience. We may have mighty physical strength, but weak in resisting temptation. The Bible gives us warnings against the dangers of self-indulgence and lack of discipline.

Dear Jesus, according to your Word I can do all things through your strength. I cast down all imaginations and every high thing that exalts itself against the knowledge of you. I bring every thought into captivity to the obedience of you. I lay aside every weight and the sin of worry, which does try so easily to beset me.

I run with patience the race that is set before me, looking unto you, the author and finisher of my faith. Amen.

Have The God Kind of Faith

Mark 11:22-24 (MEV): *Jesus answered them, Have faith in God. For truly I say to you, whoever says to this mountain, Be removed and be thrown into the sea, and does not doubt in his heart, but believes that what he says will come to pass, he will have whatever he says. Therefore I say to you, whatever things you ask when you pray, believe that you will receive them, and you will have them.*

Ephesians 2:8-9 (MEV): *For by grace you have been saved through faith, and this is not of yourselves. It is the gift of God, not of works, so that no one should boast.*

2 Thessalonians 3:2-3 (MEV): *And pray that we may be delivered from unreasonable and wicked men, for not all men have faith. But the Lord is faithful, who will establish you and guard you from the evil one.*

We can always have hope in God for wisdom and guidance to help us during difficult times. God uses all our circumstances for His Godly purposes.

We must never lose faith that God will work all things out for our good. We are precious to Him. Ultimately, at God's appointed time, He will reveal His plan for each one of us.

ABBA Father, I thank you that your ways and thoughts are above mine. I ponder your love that takes all my sorrows, sufferings, and judgment. I live accordingly, a life worthy of that love.

I thank you, Father, that you keep that which I have committed unto you. I fix my mind on those things that are true, honest, just, pure, lovely, of good report, virtuous, and deserving of praise. I will not let my heart be troubled. Amen.

Lead By Example

Ephesians 5:1-2: *Follow God's example, therefore, as dearly loved children and walk in the way of love, just as Christ loved us and gave himself up for us as a fragrant offering and sacrifice to God.*

1 Timothy 4:12: *Don't let anyone look down on you because you are young, but set an example for the believers in speech, in conduct, in love, in faith and in purity.*

Titus 2:7-8: *In everything set them an example by doing what is good. In your teaching show integrity, seriousness and soundness of speech that cannot be condemned, so that those who oppose you may be ashamed because they have nothing bad to say about us.*

We must have hope in God for direction to make the right decisions in our lives. In this world full of turmoil, we as believers should be a perfect example of love in our families, businesses, and with friends.

When we start our day with a prayer, it will make a significant impact all day long. When we have complete obedience to God, it will make a significant impact on our future.

ABBA Father, what circumstances of my life do I need to lift up to you? I lift it up even if it seems impossible to me. I abide in your word and your word abides in me. Therefore, Father, I will not forget who I am in you.

I have received the perfect law of liberty and continue therein, being not a forgetful hearer, but a doer of the Word and blessed in my doing. I thank you for the perfect example of Jesus to show me how I should live. Amen.

Your Promises Are Yes and Amen

2 Corinthians 1:20 (MEV): *For all the promises of God in Him are "Yes," and in Him "Amen," to the glory of God through us.*

2 Peter 3:13 (MEV): *But, according to His promise, we are waiting for new heavens and a new earth, in which righteousness dwells.*

1 John 2:25 (MEV): *And this is the promise that He has promised us—eternal life.*

Walking by faith is no easy task and, oftentimes, is not the choice we make. In the Bible, Abraham is presented as the supreme model of vital faith. He is the prime example of the faith required for the Christian believer. Abraham is viewed as the spiritual father for all who believe in the promises of God.

When our faith is tested like Abraham's, please remember that God is a promise keeper. He will always bless those who trust only in Him.

DEVOTIONAL

ABBA Father, today I let every desire and ambition that is not of you be surrendered and crushed. In their crushing, be filled with the oil of the Holy Spirit.

Father, teach me how to live as your faithful follower. Help me to study not merely the text of your Word but also the text of your life.

I praise you for your promises are Yes and Amen. Glory! Hallelujah!

Choices of Life

Joshua 24:15 (MSG): *If you decide that it's a bad thing to worship God, then choose a god you'd rather serve—and do it today. Choose one of the gods your ancestors worshiped from the country beyond the river, or one of the gods of the Amorites, on whose land you're now living. As for me and my family, we'll worship God.*

Proverbs 3:30-32 (NIV): *Do not accuse anyone for no reason—when they have done you no harm. Do not envy the violent or choose any of their ways. For the Lord detests the perverse but takes the upright into his confidence.*

1 Peter 1:13 (MEV): *Therefore, guard your minds, be sober, and hope to the end for the grace that is to be brought to you at the revelation of Jesus Christ.*

We must rely on God and His Word for making the right choices for our future. When we are transparent about our life mistakes and experiences it can help a loved one from making irreversible life mistakes also.

DEVOTIONAL

ABBA Father, today I fully take up my mantle in Jesus. By the power and the authority of the Holy Spirit, I step out to fulfill my calling.

Jesus, I pray that I will not be deaf to the Word you are speaking. Help me to listen and obey. As I do, remake me into your image so that my life will speak of you to those who seem deaf to your message. Father, lead me and guide me along my journey of life. Amen.

God's Word Is Truth

Romans 15:4 (MEV): *For whatever was previously written was written for our instruction, so that through perseverance and encouragement of the Scriptures we might have hope.*

2 Timothy 3:16-17 (MEV): *All Scripture is inspired by God and is profitable for teaching, for reproof, for correction, and for instruction in righteousness, that the man of God may be complete, thoroughly equipped for every good work.*

Hebrews 4:12 (MEV): *For the word of God is alive, and active, and sharper than any two-edged sword, piercing even to the division of soul and spirit, of joints and marrow, and able to judge the thoughts and intents of the heart.*

When we have a close and personal relationship with God, it is so important to imitate His character. It is imperative to study and meditate on God's Word. A lack of knowledge and wrong interpretations of His Word can cause division in our relationships.

ABBA Father, today I pause, stop what I am doing, cease from my routine and my course, and, with no preconceptions, seek you. Father, help me to be a brilliant and awesome light just for you today. I let your Word dwell in me richly.

He who began a good work in me will continue until the return of Christ Jesus. I need discernment to rightly divide Your Word and cause no offense. Amen.

Follow the Leader

Exodus 18:21-22 (KJV): *Moreover thou shalt provide out of all the people able men, such as fear God, men of truth, hating covetousness; and place such over them, to be rulers of thousands, and rulers of hundreds, rulers of fifties, and rulers of tens: And let them judge the people at all seasons: and it shall be, that every great matter they shall bring unto thee, but every small matter they shall judge: so shall it be easier for thyself, and they shall bear the burden with thee.*

Ephesians 4:11-16 (KJV): *And he gave some, apostles; and some, prophets; and some, evangelists; and some, pastors and teachers; For the perfecting of the saints, for the work of the ministry, for the edifying of the body of Christ: Till we all come in the unity of the faith, and of the knowledge of the Son of God, unto a perfect man, unto the measure of the stature of the fulness of Christ: That we henceforth be no more children, tossed to and fro, and carried about with every wind of doctrine, by the sleight of men, and cunning craftiness, whereby they lie in wait to deceive; But speaking the truth in love, may grow up into him in all things, which is the head, even Christ: From whom the whole body fitly joined together and compacted by that which every joint supplieth, according to the effectual working in the measure of every part, maketh increase of the body unto the edifying of itself in love.*

Colossians 1:23 (KJV): *If ye continue in the faith grounded and settled and be not moved away from the hope of the Gospel, which ye have heard, and which was preached to every creature which is under heaven; whereof I Paul am made a minister.*

Those who are in a leadership position have an extra responsibility to honor God. God expects those He puts in leadership positions to humble themselves. Jealousy and pride stand in the way of fellowship with God. Those traits also prevent God from using His leaders to minister to others. We are to rejoice in the gifts God gives us and use them carefully. Let us focus on Christ's example of love and acceptance of others.

ABBA Father, I live this day, not by my old calendar but by the calendar in which every day and every moment is new.

Father, I pray for the right timing and the right circumstances to follow through with the goals we have set together. Help me to be awake to the possibilities and open to the direction you would take me. I will honor you by carefully using my gifts for your kingdom. Amen.

Mountain Moving Faith

Matthew 17:20 (MEV): *Jesus said to them, "Because of your unbelief. For truly I say to you, if you have faith as a grain of mustard seed, you will say to this mountain, 'Move from here to there,' and it will move. And nothing will be impossible for you."*

Mark 11:23-25 (MEV): *For truly I say to you, whoever says to this mountain, 'Be removed and be thrown into the sea,' and does not doubt in his heart, but believes that what he says will come to pass, he will have whatever he says. Therefore I say to you, whatever things you ask when you pray, believe that you will receive them, and you will have them. And when you stand praying, forgive if you have anything against anyone, so that your Father who is in heaven may also forgive you your sins.*

2 Thessalonians 2:16-17 (MEV): *Now may our Lord Jesus Christ Himself, and God our Father, who has loved us and has given us eternal consolation and good hope through grace, comfort your hearts and establish you in every good word and work.*

We can have hope in God giving us instructions on how to be a good provider for our families and planning for the future. Having hope and faith in God means not relying on our present circumstances.

Always remember f.e.a.r. (false evidence appearing real) is the total opposite of faith. The Lord views fear as a lack of faith in His promises. Let us follow the example of Joshua and Caleb, who had faith in God and lived to possess their divine inheritance.

DEVOTIONAL

ABBA Father, instead of struggling to accomplish your will, help me to live and be moved by the Holy Spirit.

Father, it overwhelms me to realize that you have chosen me. Help me to trust you and grow in faith for your glory. Thank you for my measure of faith that I can move mountains. Amen.

Choices Have Consequences

Proverbs 10:28-29 (MEV): *The hope of the righteous will be gladness, but the expectation of the wicked will perish. The way of the Lord is strength to the upright, but destruction will come to the workers of iniquity.*

Galatians 6:7-9 (MEV): *Be not deceived. God is not mocked. For whatever a man sows, that will he also reap. For the one who sows to his own flesh will from the flesh reap corruption, but the one who sows to the Spirit will from the Spirit reap eternal life. And let us not grow weary in doing good, for in due season we shall reap, if we do not give up.*

Colossians 3:23-25 (MEV): *And whatever you do, do it heartily, as for the Lord and not for men, knowing that from the Lord you will receive the reward of the inheritance. For you serve the Lord Christ. But he who does wrong will receive for the wrong which he has done, and there is no partiality.*

When under stress, we may be tempted to do something we would never consider under normal circumstances. However, it is never right to do wrong.

Ambition can be a positive thing if we do not disregard other people to achieve success. Whenever we consider doing wrong to achieve a personal goal, remember that choices have a domino effect on the lives of those around us.

DEVOTIONAL

ABBA Father, I thank you for the Holy B.I.B.L.E (Basic Instructions Before Leaving Earth) to help me make the right choices in life.

Today I stay as far away from temptation as I can and as close as I can to you. Far from the wolf (Satan) and near to the Good Shepherd, Jesus Christ.

Father, let your power flow through me today so that I handle everything with trust and joy. Amen.

Attitude Determines Altitude

Luke 10:38-42 (ERV): *While Jesus and his followers were traveling, he went into a town, and a woman named Martha let him stay at her house. She had a sister named Mary. Mary was sitting at Jesus' feet and listening to him teach. But her sister Martha was busy doing all the work that had to be done. Martha went in and said, "Lord, don't you care that my sister has left me to do all the work by myself? Tell her to help me!" But the Lord answered her, "Martha, Martha, you are getting worried and upset about too many things. Only one thing is important. Mary has made the right choice, and it will never be taken away from her."*

Romans 15:4-6 (CEB): *Whatever was written in the past was written for our instruction so that we could have hope through endurance and through the encouragement of the scriptures. May the God of endurance and encouragement give you the same attitude toward each other, similar to Christ Jesus' attitude. That way you can glorify the God and Father of our Lord Jesus Christ together with one voice.*

Ephesians 4:22-24 (NIV): *You were taught, with regard to your former way of life, to put off your old self, which is being corrupted by its deceitful desires; to be made new in the attitude of your minds; and to put on the new self, created to be like God in true righteousness and holiness.*

All those who mistreat us, even the evil people we meet, have a role in God's plan. This is important to remember when we encounter people that cause unjust suffering. We can still trust God, knowing that He is with us. We can still expect God to use our every experience to shape us for something in our future. We also can pity our persecutors, who mean to do us evil but are unaware God will use it for our good.

DEVOTIONAL

ABBA Father, I remove from my life today, any action or thought which lead to death, starting with sin. I replace them with that which leads to life.

There are times I do not know what I ought to pray for. Holy Spirit, I submit to your leadership and thank you for interceding for me. You search my heart and know my mind and my spirit because you intercede for me in accordance with Father's will. Therefore, I am assured and know that with God being a partner in my labor, all things work together and are fitting into a plan for my good, because I love God and I am called according to His design and purpose.

I am so grateful that You will never leave me nor forsake me. Amen.

God Can Use a Few Good Warriors

Deuteronomy 20:1-4 (MEV): *When you go out to battle against your enemies, and see horses, and chariots, and a people that outnumber you, do not be afraid of them, for the Lord your God is with you, who brought you up out of the land of Egypt. It will be, when you approach the battle, that the priest will approach and speak to the people, and he shall say to them, "Hear, O Israel, you approach today to do battle against your enemies. Do not be fainthearted. Do not fear, and do not tremble or be terrified because of them. For the Lord, your God is He that goes with you, to fight for you against your enemies, to save you."*

Zechariah 10:5 (MEV): *And they will be as mighty men, who trample down in the muddy streets in battle. They will fight because the Lord is with them, and He will put to shame those riding on horses.*

Romans 8:37-39 (ISV): *In all these things we are triumphantly victorious due to the one who loved us. For I am convinced that neither death, nor life, nor angels, nor rulers, nor things present, nor things to come, nor powers, nor anything above, nor anything below, nor anything else in all creation can separate us from the love of God that is ours in union with the Messiah Jesus, our Lord.*

Oftentimes, we may feel like we are the least to achieve anything great. One choice to obey and have hope in God can change your life or maybe an entire nation. God calls leaders for His divine service from unlikely situations and places. He needs dedicated and disciplined followers. We can rely on the power of God even when circumstances and common sense might dictate another course of action.

ABBA Father, I move forward this day in the power of Jesus, through every veil, wall, separation, and hindrance.

ABBA Father, thank you for sending your Son as my Savior. Oh, how I praise you for granting me the faith to believe! You rescued me from my sin. You died to save me. You love me so much. I am undeserving of Your great love.

Help my life to demonstrate to the world that you are Jesus, my Savior. Help me never to be ashamed of you and let me be ever willing to shout from the rooftops that you are the only God. Help me to never grab at the honor and glory that belongs to you. Amen.

A Christian Life

Romans 12:9-13 (MEV): *Let love be without hypocrisy. Hate what is evil. Cleave to what is good. Be devoted to one another with brotherly love; prefer one another in honor, do not be lazy in diligence, be fervent in spirit, serve the Lord, rejoice in hope, be patient in suffering, persevere in prayer, contribute to the needs of the saints, practice hospitality.*

2 Corinthians 5:17-19 (MEV): *Therefore, if any man is in Christ, he is a new creature. Old things have passed away. Look, all things have become new. All this is from God, who has reconciled us to Himself through Jesus Christ and has given to us the ministry of reconciliation, that is, that God was in Christ reconciling the world to Himself, not counting their sins against them, and has entrusted to us the message of reconciliation.*

Galatians 3:26-28 (MEV): *You are all sons of God by faith in Christ Jesus. For as many of you as have been baptized into Christ have put on Christ. There is neither Jew nor Greek, there is neither slave nor free, and there is neither male nor female, for you are all one in Christ Jesus.*

We as Christians must demonstrate to the world what a hard-working businessperson truly looks like. Our character should reflect people of faith who are wise in providing for our families. Also, be an example of kindness and caring for others.

DEVOTIONAL

ABBA Father, is there something in my life that you have called me to do that I have not yet done? I will do it today.

Father, help me be willing to light a candle anywhere that seems dark. Bless the people around me with your precious light. It is my desire to be more Christ-like and lift you up in front of men. Amen.

Make Godly Decisions

Proverbs 3:5-6 (MEV): *Trust in the Lord with all your heart and lean not on your own understanding; in all your ways acknowledge Him, and He will direct your paths.*

Proverbs 16:9-11 (NCV): *People may make plans in their minds, but the LORD decides what they will do. The words of a king are like a message from God, so his decisions should be fair. The LORD wants honest balances and scales; all the weights are his work.*

Isaiah 10:1-2 (NASB): *Woe to those who enact evil statutes and to those who constantly record unjust decisions, so as to deprive the needy of justice and rob the poor of My people of their rights, so that widows may be their spoil and that they may plunder the orphans.*

Oftentimes, we make decisions with no consideration for the consequences they will have on our families or others. We must not seek riches and a life of ease rather than a path of obedience to God.

Pursuing the comforts and customs of this wicked world will separate us from God. But if we follow God and His Word and lean not to our own understanding, we will have a victorious and abundant life.

ABBA Father, I live this day in confidence and hope, looking to the future, knowing You are already there. You are the Father of my future and you are waiting for me to arrive.

Help me to seek you in all I do and to choose to have the best day possible. Today, I decree that I will lean not to my understanding but to rely on your Word. Amen.

We Are Family

Psalm 133:1 (MEV): *Behold, how good and how pleasant it is for brothers to dwell together in unity!*

Acts 16:31-34 (MEV): *They said, Believe in the Lord Jesus Christ, and you and your household will be saved. And they spoke the word of the Lord to him and to all who were in his household. In that hour of the night he took them and washed their wounds. And immediately he and his entire household were baptized. Then he brought them up to his house and set food before them. And he rejoiced with his entire household believing in God.*

1 John 4:19-21 (MEV): *We love Him because He first loved us. If anyone says, "I love God," and hates his brother, he is a liar. For whoever does not love his brother whom he has seen, how can he love God whom he has not seen? We have this commandment from Him: Whoever loves God must also love his brother.*

Jesus sees promise in all of us that He called to be His disciple. As a follower of Jesus Christ, we are now in a family of privilege. It is our commission to use this privilege to help and lead others to Jesus.

The Word was made flesh and dwelt among us and His name is Jesus!

Dear Jesus, I love You. Your name and your word are exalted above all else. I embrace and magnify your word. Hallowed be thy name!

I thank you for your sacrifice at Calvary. Thank you for adopting me into your heavenly family. I do not fear the battles; that which is good is worth fighting for. When I fight the good fight of faith, I will prevail. Amen.

Show The Love Of God

Colossians 3:13-15 (MEV): *Bear with one another and forgive one another. If anyone has a quarrel against anyone, even as Christ forgave you, so you must do. And above all these things, embrace love, which is the bond of perfection. Let the peace of God, to which also you are called in one body, rule in your hearts. And be thankful.*

1 Peter 4:8-9 (MEV): *Above all things, have unfailing love for one another, because love covers a multitude of sins. Show hospitality to one another without complaining.*

1 John 4:7-8 (MEV): *Beloved, let us love one another, for love is of God, and everyone who loves is born of God and knows God. Anyone who does not love does not know God, for God is love.*

There is always a chance for reconciliation when we continue to show love. Whether we are trying to reconcile with a family member, friend, or business partner, his or her best interest should be considered.

Taking matters into our own hands and seeking revenge can only have a negative outcome. God says vengeance is His only.

ABBA Father, I need help with showing love when I have been mistreated. Help me to overcome fear, worry, and anxiety. Please help me to trust and throw my cares upon you.

ABBA Father, I pray your will be done in my life as it is in Heaven. For I am your handiwork, recreated in Christ Jesus, that I may do the good works that you predestined for me to do. I will walk in them, living the good life that you predestined and fashioned for me to live. Amen.

World Changers

Matthew 5:14-16 (MEV): *You are the light of the world. A city that is set on a hill cannot be hidden. Neither do men light a candle and put it under a basket, but on a candlestick. And it gives light to all who are in the house. Let your light so shine before men that they may see your good works and glorify your Father who is in heaven.*

John 13:34-35 (MEV): *A new commandment I give to you, that you love one another, even as I have loved you, that you also love one another. By this all men will know that you are My disciples, if you have love for one another.*

Romans 12:1-3 (MEV): *I urge you therefore, brothers, by the mercies of God, that you present your bodies as a living sacrifice, holy, and acceptable to God, which is your reasonable service of worship. Do not be conformed to this world, but be transformed by the renewing of your mind, that you may prove what is the good and acceptable and perfect will of God. For I say, through the grace given to me, to everyone among you, not to think of himself more highly than he ought to think, but to think with sound judgment, according to the measure of faith God has distributed to every man.*

We as men and women of God must make it a lifestyle to seek His guidance daily. Let us remember that it is not a job, title, or position that can change any crisis but being a living epistle of the Word of God.

With the love of God, let us oppose the accepted standards and norms of this present age which accepts other gods. As a living epistle of the Word of God, we affect the world.

DEVOTIONAL

ABBA Father, I choose today to be a living epistle of your Word to affect the world. I will be fruitful. Where there is no fruit of love or hope, forgiveness, or joy, I will be the first one to bear them.

Father, I thank you for teaching me to be loving and kind. Help me to honor acts of kindness in others today. Amen.

I Got A Testimony

Mark 5:19-20 (NIRV): *Jesus did not let him. He said, "Go home to your own people. Tell them how much the Lord has done for you. Tell them how kind he has been to you." So the man went away. In the area known as the Ten Cities, he began to tell how much Jesus had done for him. And all the people were amazed.*

John 15:26-27 (HCSB): *When the Counselor comes, the One I will send to you from the Father—the Spirit of truth who proceeds from the Father—He will testify about Me. You also will testify because you have been with Me from the beginning.*

1 Peter 3:15 (MEV): *But sanctify the Lord God in your hearts. Always be ready to give an answer to every man who asks you for a reason for the hope that is in you, with gentleness and fear.*

Oftentimes, we feel our way is better than God and then consequences prove differently. However, our obedience may lead us to our purpose in life or ministry.

An important lesson to learn is not to judge God's ultimate intentions for our lives based on current circumstances. We do not want to be like the prodigal son who had to hit rock bottom to remind him of the hope and love which is found in God. God will always turn our mess into a message if we surrender our will to Him.

As we share our testimony about the goodness of God and all that He has done for us, it will help others. We are more than conquerors through Christ Jesus.

ABBA Father, I take all my sins and all that oppresses me and cast it onto the cross. Teach me to do your will, for you are my ABBA God.

Let your Good Spirit lead me. Jesus, you gave yourself up for my sins in order to rescue and deliver me from the present and wicked age in accordance with the will, purpose, and plan of our ABBA God.

I thank you for my testimony to share with others about the tests you brought me through. Amen.

God Loves Prodigals

Isaiah 43:5-6 (VOICE): *So don't be afraid. I am here. I will reunite you with your children, bringing them back from wherever in the world they are—East, West, North, or South. No place will be able to hold you when I demand your release, when I order them, Bring My children—My sons and daughters—from far away.*

Matthew 18:12-13 (VOICE): *A shepherd in charge of 100 sheep notices that one of his sheep has gone astray. What do you think he should do? Should the shepherd leave the flock on the hills unguarded to search for the lost sheep? God's shepherd goes to look for that one lost sheep, and when he finds her, he is happier about her return than he is about the 99 who stayed put.*

Luke 15:20-24 (VOICE): *So he got up and returned to his father. The father looked off in the distance and saw the young man returning. He felt compassion for his son and ran out to him, enfolded him in an embrace, and kissed him. The son said, "Father, I have done a terrible wrong in God's sight and in your sight too. I have forfeited any right to be treated as your son." But the father turned to his servants and said, "Quick! Bring the best robe we have and put it on him. Put a ring on his finger and shoes on his feet. Go get the fattest calf and butcher it. Let's have a feast and celebrate because my son was dead and is alive again. He was lost and has been found." So they had this huge party.*

When Jesus told the parable of two sons, He devoted the first part of the story to the younger son who was reckless, extravagant and lost all his possessions. The lesson of the prodigal son is that when one abandons his father's house to venture into the far country, he ends up with empty pockets, an empty stomach, and a starving soul. This parable conveys the attitude of forgiveness that God expresses to those who repent of their sins. Our Heavenly Father embraces His prodigal children with unconditional love and forgiveness and restores them into the family.

ABBA Father, I thank you for never giving up on me when I was in that far country away from you. Thank you that Christ has become my defense attorney, therefore, today I start living a judgment and condemnation-free life.

Father, help me to create the best possible life by making choices that please you and that bring me closer to being all that I can be for you. Amen.

Do You Believe in Miracles?

Job 5:8-9: *But if I were you, I would appeal to God; I would lay my cause before him. He performs wonders that cannot be fathomed, miracles that cannot be counted.*

Acts 19:11-12: *God did extraordinary miracles through Paul, so that even handkerchiefs and aprons that had touched him were taken to the sick, and their illnesses were cured, and the evil spirits left them.*

Hebrews 2:4: *God also testified to it by signs, wonders and various miracles, and by gifts of the Holy Spirit distributed according to his will.*

There are several people in the Bible who received a miracle from God. I will mention only two.

The Shunammite woman and Hannah were women who longed to have children. Each received their miracle sons through the power of prayer. These miracles demonstrated that God is the God of the impossible for those who chose to believe.

Many times, the answers to our prayers do not come right away, but a delay is not a denial. God has His appointed time for all His promises.

ABBA Father, I take a word from Scripture, dwell on it, agree with it, and bind it to my thoughts, my emotions, my heart, and my mind.

Father, thank you for enriching my life with your presence and creating a unique purpose for me. Help me to truly make a difference in the lives of others. I am grateful that you are faithful to your promises. Amen! Glory! Hallelujah!

Our Hope Is In God

Psalm 146:5-6 (MEV): *Blessed is he who has the God of Jacob for his help, whose hope is in the Lord his God.*

Jeremiah 14:22 (NIV): *Do any of the worthless idols of the nations bring rain? Do the skies themselves send down showers? No, it is you, LORD our God. Therefore our hope is in you, for you are the one who does all this.*

Romans 15:13 (MEV): *Now may the God of hope fill you with all joy and peace in believing, so that you may abound in hope, through the power of the Holy Spirit.*

Oftentimes, we can be satisfied with our current life circumstances. We may reason with ourselves, *if I want nothing, I cannot suffer from its lack. If I have nothing, I cannot be hurt by its loss.* However, such a life is empty.

For those who have tried to isolate themselves from hurt by determining not to dream, the sudden introduction of hope can be overwhelming. Do not choose to live a life without hope but trust in the God that gives hope. God invites us to live in hope and expectation rather than hopelessness.

While it is true that living in hope may bring us an unexpected pain and that every gain brings with it the possibility of loss, our God who guards and guides us is gracious indeed. In opening our lives to whatever the future can be, our hope will bear much fruit.

ABBA Father, I live today in a state of thoroughness. I make you my Alpha, the reason for everything I do, and my Omega, the one for whom I live.

ABBA Father, in love, you predestined me unto the adoption as a child by Jesus Christ to yourself, according to the good pleasure of your will. Your will be done on earth in my life as it is in Heaven. Amen! Glory! Hallelujah!

God Hears Our Prayers

Psalm 141:1-2 (KJ21): *Lord, I cry unto Thee! Make haste unto me! Give ear unto my voice when I cry unto Thee. Let my prayer be set before Thee as incense, and the lifting up of my hands as the evening sacrifice.*

Jeremiah 29:12-13 (KJ21): *Then shall ye call upon Me, and ye shall go and pray unto Me and I will hearken unto you. And ye shall seek Me and find Me when ye shall search for Me with all your heart.*

Mark 11:24 (KJ21): *Therefore I say unto you, what things so ever ye desire when ye pray, believe that ye receive them, and ye shall have them.*

Throughout history, Hannah has been honored both as Prophet Samuel's mother and as a woman of faith. Hannah's life portrays how setting our hearts on something we do not have can rob us of appreciation for the gifts God has given us. It was only when Hannah surrendered the object of her desire to God that she found release from her anguish and discovered peace.

ABBA Father, today I build and place my tent of meeting with you in the center of my day and life. I place the rest of my day and life around it. I thank you for hearing me when I pray.

Father, I want to be the real me in every area of my life. I especially want to be authentic in my relationship with you. Amen.

In God I Trust

Psalm 28:6-7: *Praise be to the Lord, for he has heard my cry for mercy. The Lord is my strength and my shield; my heart trusts in him, and he helps me. My heart leaps for joy, and with my song I praise him.*

Proverbs 3:5-6: *Trust in the Lord with all your heart and lean not on your own understanding; in all your ways submit to him, and he will make your paths straight.*

Isaiah 26:3-4: *You will keep in perfect peace those whose minds are steadfast, because they trust in you. Trust in the Lord forever, for the Lord, the Lord himself, is the Rock eternal.*

As we look at the big picture in our world today, we see hopeless situations. When we take away hope, even the small things crush us. Is this how God intended us to live? Is this the kind of life He created us for?

Thankfully, the answer is no. Instead, the Word of God shows us that the same events or experiences we have right now are like many Biblical characters. We can learn from their testaments and testimonies that there is hope when we trust in God.

ABBA Father, what is it that I am meant to do and be in my life? Help me to take steps today to fulfill my calling.

ABBA, thank you for good health, food, clothing, and shelter. In the name of Jesus, I am learning to stop being anxious and worried about my life. I thank you for being my God of hope. I trust you and your Word to lead and guide me. Amen.

The Cross

Philippians 2:8 (MEV): *And being found in the form of a man, He humbled Himself and became obedient to death, even death on a cross.*

Colossians 1:19-20 (MEV): *For it pleased the Father that in Him all fullness should dwell, and to reconcile all things to Himself by Him, having made peace through the blood of His cross, by Him, I say—whether they are things in earth, or things in heaven.*

Hebrews 12:2 (MEV): *Let us look to Jesus, the author and finisher of our faith, who for the joy that was set before Him endured the cross, despising the shame, and is seated at the right hand of the throne of God.*

One of the major significance of the cross after Jesus' death and resurrection is its use as a symbol of Jesus' willingness to suffer for our sins so that we might be reconciled to God. The cross, then, is the symbol of Jesus' love, God's power to save, and the thankful believer's unreserved commitment to Christian discipleship. To those who know the salvation that Christ gained for us through His death, it is a wondrous cross indeed.

Dear Jesus, I bring my life totally to the cross. It is a doorway. I use its access to go where I never could go before.

Father, help me and guide me into all truth. I thank you for your loving sacrifice that was shown on the cross. Amen.

My Heart Longs

1 Samuel 16:7 (MEV): *But the Lord said to Samuel, "Do not look on his appearance or on the height of his stature, because I have rejected him. For the Lord sees not as man sees. For man looks on the outward appearance, but the Lord looks on the heart."*

Psalm 119:81-82 (TPT): *I'm lovesick with yearnings for more of your salvation, for my heart is entwined with your word. I'm consumed with longings for your promises, so I ask, "When will they all come true?"*

Jeremiah 17:10 (MEV): *I, the Lord, search the heart, I test the mind, even to give to every man according to his ways, and according to the fruit of his deeds.*

In the Bible, the word *heart* has a much broader meaning than it does to the modern mind. By the world's standards, outward beauty is what matters most. But God looks and reacts to the inner beauty of our *hearts*.

Oftentimes, it is good to have someone in our lives that we can express what is on our minds and in our hearts. Someone who will sincerely listen when we are talking to them. Someone who is an encourager, especially during the difficult times in our lives.

It is a must to not let disappointments of our past dictate our future or destiny. Whatever test or trial we may be going through, there is a testimony to share, encourage, and give hope to someone else.

ABBA Father, my heart longs to hear your voice just as Jesus did. Help me to draw away from this frantic and busy world to be alone with you.

I remember all the times of my life when you turned my sorrows into blessings. Open my eyes to see what you want to show me, my ears to hear what you desire to tell me. Help me to know what to pray in secret as I respond to your heart.

Father, I give you the glory and thank you for giving me a chance to start another new day. Amen.

Children Are a Blessing

Psalm 127:3-4 (MEV): *Look, children are a gift of the LORD, and the fruit of the womb is a reward. As arrows in the hand of a mighty warrior, so are the children of one's youth.*

Mark 19:13-15 (MEV): *Then little children were brought to Him that He might put His hands on them and pray. But the disciples rebuked them. But Jesus said, "Let the little children come to Me, and do not forbid them. For to such belongs the kingdom of heaven." He laid His hands on them and departed from there.*

Luke 9:47-48 (MEV): *Jesus, perceiving the thought of their heart, took a child and put him by Him, and said to them, "Whoever receives this child in My name receives Me, and whoever receives Me receives Him who sent Me. For he who is least among you all will be great."*

There are approximately two billion children in this world and so many of the two billion are living lives of abuse and neglect. Children are the most helpless members of the human race, dependent upon others for food, physical safety, and emotional comfort. They cannot demand these rights.

A child has the right to be loved and accepted. A child can detect a lack of compassion and affection early in life. Let us remember that our Lord and Savior chose to come to earth and start life as an infant. As we celebrate Jesus, please remember the two billion children in this world.

Dear Jesus, give me a burden for children in my neighborhood, city, nation, and the world and increase my faith to intercede for them. Bring others near to pray with me for this generation of children and young people. I ask that you would raise up workers so that children who are starving physically, emotionally, or spiritually, would find all their needs met in you. Amen.

Show Compassion

Zechariah 7:9-10: *"This is what the Lord Almighty said: 'Administer true justice; show mercy and compassion to one another. Do not oppress the widow or the fatherless, the foreigner or the poor. Do not plot evil against each other.'"*

Philippians 2:1-4: *Therefore if you have any encouragement from being united with Christ, if any comfort from his love, if any common sharing in the Spirit, if any tenderness and compassion, then make my joy complete by being like-minded, having the same love, being one in spirit and of one mind. Do nothing out of selfish ambition or vain conceit. Rather, in humility value others above yourselves, not looking to your own interests but each of you to the interests of the others.*

Colossians 3:12-13: *Therefore, as God's chosen people, holy and dearly loved, clothe yourselves with compassion, kindness, humility, gentleness, and patience. Bear with each other and forgive one another if any of you has a grievance against someone. Forgive as the Lord forgave you.*

One of the perfect examples of love is giving back to our communities. Showing compassion and kindness for people can be a legacy that inspires others to live in the same way. Doing good to someone comes back to you. We must influence others to enjoy the best of life. Life is just a short visit – do not hurry or worry.

Dear Jesus, I commit to becoming a vessel of giving, to fully show compassion. I start today and my life will become the reflection of you. Bring to remembrance people I have forgotten and those you would have me intercede for or provide for.

When I make a commitment or a promise to someone, please help me to fulfill it quickly so that I don't forget to do it. Remind me often that you never fail to show compassion to me. Amen.

Victory Is Mine

Deuteronomy 20:3-4: *He shall say: "Hear, Israel: Today you are going into battle against your enemies. Do not be fainthearted or afraid; do not panic or be terrified by them. For the Lord, your God is the one who goes with you to fight for you against your enemies to give you victory."*

Proverbs 21:30-31: *There is no wisdom, no insight, no plan that can succeed against the Lord. The horse is made ready for the day of battle, but victory rests with the Lord.*

1 Corinthians 15:57: *But thanks be to God! He gives us the victory through our Lord Jesus Christ.*

The Book of Esther shows how God has kept His promise of deliverance throughout history. Just as Haman met his death by execution, we can trust God to protect us from the enemy, Satan, and to work out His ultimate purpose of redemption in our lives.

A careful reading will reveal that the Book of Esther teaches a valuable lesson about the sovereignty of God. Although the enemies of the Covenant people may triumph for a season, God holds the key to ultimate victory.

Dear Jesus, whatever good I would do, I do it now. I treat this day as if it comes around once in eternity because it does.

Jesus, according to Matthew 5:44, you said, *Love your enemies and pray for those who persecute you.* **I come before you to lift up my enemies. I invoke blessings upon them and pray for their happiness. I implore your blessings and favor upon them. Thank you for victory over my enemies. Amen.**

Do You Know The Truth?

Psalm 25:4-5 (MEV): *Make me to know Your ways, O Lord; teach me Your paths. Lead me in Your truth and teach me, for You are the God of my salvation; on You I wait all the day.*

Zechariah 8:15-17 (MEV): *So again have I purposed in these days to do good to Jerusalem and to the house of Judah. Do not fear! These are the things you will do: Speak truth each to his neighbor and make judgments in your gates that are for truth, and justice, and peace. Let none of you consider evil plans in your heart against your neighbor, and do not love false oaths, for I hate all these things, says the Lord.*

1 John 3:17-19 (MEV): *Whoever has the world's goods and sees his brother in need, but closes his heart of compassion from him, how can the love of God remain in him? My little children, let us love not in word and speech, but in action and truth. By this we know that we are of the truth and shall reassure our hearts before Him.*

A daily study of the Bible can help develop problem-solving skills and teach the value of seeking God in our daily decision-making. The Bible can help us cope with stress and a variety of emotional and behavioral issues with our families, co-workers, etc. Seeking godly counseling may help also to discuss feelings about family issues, particularly if there is a major transition such as a divorce, move, or serious illness.

DEVOTIONAL

ABBA Father, today I let the Gospel produce your acts in my life. I let all my acts proceed from the Good News. I get wholly into the Bible and I will enter the Book of Acts.

Loving ABBA, help me not to judge your love for me be based on whether today brings good or bad news. Help me remember that you desire to use my circumstances to make me more like Jesus. Thank you for your Word and please give me clarity and wisdom to be able to apply it to my life. Amen.

Depend On Jesus

Psalm 27:13-14 (MEV): *I believe I will see the goodness of the Lord in the land of the living. Wait on the Lord; be strong, and may your heart be stout; wait on the Lord.*

Proverbs 3:5-6 (MEV): *Trust in the Lord with all your heart and lean not on your own understanding; in all your ways acknowledge Him, and He will direct your paths.*

Hebrews 6:19-20 (MEV): *We have this hope as a sure and steadfast anchor of the soul, which enters the Inner Place behind the veil. This is where Jesus has entered for us as a forerunner since He has become the everlasting High Priest in the order of Melchizedek.*

Significant life events such as the death of a family member or friend, divorce or a move, abuse, trauma, or a major illness in the family can cause stress that might lead to problems with mood, sleep, appetite, and social functioning. However, with Jesus, we can persevere. No matter what circumstances are surrounding us, we can always depend on Jesus to be our anchor of hope.

Dear Jesus, thank you that Heaven is not only after this life but within it. I live this day as the commencement of a Heavenly life, the beginning of Heaven. My desire is to be an imitator of you.

Through you, Jesus, I can do all things because you strengthen me. Jesus, I am grateful that I have great peace in my current circumstances. I refuse to take offense of my enemies. Thank you for being my anchor to keep my mind, my will, and my emotions steady. Amen.

Restored World

Acts 3:19-21 (MEV): *Therefore repent and be converted, that your sins may be wiped away, that times of refreshing may come from the presence of the Lord, and that He may send the One who previously was preached to you, Jesus Christ, whom the heavens must receive until the time of restoring what God spoke through all His holy prophets since the world began.*

2 Corinthians 13:11-12 (ESV): *Finally, brothers, rejoice. Aim for restoration, comfort one another, agree with one another, live in peace; and the God of love and peace will be with you. Greet one another with a holy kiss.*

1 Peter 5:10 (MEV): *But after you have suffered a little while, the God of all grace, who has called us to His eternal glory through Christ Jesus, will restore, support, strengthen, and establish you.*

Oftentimes, it can be disheartening when we are judged by social status, race, gender, and any other way we might be different than others. But God has spoken in His Word that one day His children will live together, everyone will respect each other and look out for one another. There will be no social divisions. God will restore this world to His beautiful original intentions.

ABBA Father, help me to see everyone through your loving eyes. I dwell in Heaven's Outer Court, the place of sacrifice. Therefore, the life I live here must be one of sacrifice, a life of love begins today.

Father, please protect my love relationships. Help me to be the kind of person that makes it easy for others to relate to me in loving ways. Help me to be patient and kind to everyone today. Amen.

Random Acts of Kindness

Proverbs 3:3-4 (NLV): *Do not let kindness and truth leave you. Tie them around your neck. Write them upon your heart. So you will find favor and good understanding in the eyes of God and man.*

Acts 9:36 (NLV): *A woman who was a follower lived in the city of Joppa. Her name was Tabitha, or Dorcas. She did many good things and many acts of kindness.*

2 Peter 1:5-8 (NIRV): *So you should try very hard to add goodness to your faith. To goodness, add knowledge. To knowledge, add the ability to control yourselves. To the ability to control yourselves, add the strength to keep going. To the strength to keep going, add godliness. To godliness, add kindness for one another. And to kindness for one another, add love. All these things should describe you more and more. They will make you useful and fruitful as you know our Lord Jesus Christ better.*

One of the main reasons for time is so all of life does not happen at once. Let us make time to spend it with the ones we love. Kind words are the oil that keeps the friction out of life. Always remember to never underestimate the power of a touch, a smile, a sweet word, a listening ear, an honest compliment, or an act of kindness. Any one of these has the potential to turn a life around.

ABBA Father, thank you for loving me and showing me how to love those close to me. I show my love, I forgive, and I bless. I will not wait because today is the day of the harvest and I will share the Good News.

Father, I do not understand all that goes on around me, but I thank you for keeping me grounded in your love and in my faith. Amen.

Love

Leviticus 19:17-18 (MEV): *You shall not hate your brother in your heart. You shall surely reason honestly with your neighbor, and not suffer sin because of him. You shall not take vengeance, nor bear any grudge against the children of your people, but you shall love your neighbor as yourself: I am the Lord.*

John 13:34-35 (MEV): *A new commandment I give to you, that you love one another, even as I have loved you, that you also love one another. By this all men will know that you are My disciples, if you have love for one another.*

1 John 4:20-21 (MEV): *If anyone says, "I love God," and hates his brother, he is a liar. For whoever does not love his brother whom he has seen, how can he love God whom he has not seen? We have this commandment from Him: Whoever loves God must also love his brother.*

A day should not go by that we do not show our spouse or loved ones some type of affection. Married couples should show the world how to love by not arguing or raising their voices in public. The secret to any lasting relationship is respect for one another and good communication. However, when you do have a disagreement, never go to bed angry; find a mutual compromise. Tomorrow is not promised, so we must cherish the time we have today and our loved ones.

ABBA Father, I ponder those events of my life over which I had no peace. I will be at peace and give thanks that you will work all these things for my good. I endure everything without weakening because your love in me never fails.

ABBA, I commit to walking in your love with my family and friends. Amen.

The Great Commandment

Zephaniah 3:17 (MEV): *The Lord your God is in your midst, a Mighty One, who will save. He will rejoice over you with gladness, He will renew you with His love, He will rejoice over you with singing.*

Mark 12:30-31 (MEV): *You shall love the Lord your God with all your heart, and with all your soul, and with all your mind, and with all your strength. This is the first commandment. The second is this: You shall love your neighbor as yourself. There is no other commandment greater than these.*

1 John 4:7-12 (MEV): *Beloved, let us love one another, for love is of God, and everyone who loves is born of God and knows God. Anyone who does not love does not know God, for God is love. In this way the love of God was revealed to us, that God sent His only begotten Son into the world, that we might live through Him. In this is love: not that we loved God, but that He loved us and sent His Son to be the atoning sacrifice for our sins. Beloved, if God so loved us, we must also love one another. No one has seen God at any time. If we love one another, God dwells in us, and His love is perfected in us.*

God created mankind to have a personal relationship with Him and then with each other. God's **commandment**, not suggestion, is to love Him with all our soul, mind, and body. Only then can we love one another.

Oftentimes, we have people in our lives that need to learn how to love us. We as believers must live a life different from this world of self-centeredness. As the children of the Most High God, let us lead by example and care about others.

ABBA Father, help me be a constant flow of love to everyone I encounter. I bring the most ungodly, dark, and untouched part of my life to you.

ABBA, thank you for making me your child. Help me to be confident of your love, despite my failings, so confident that I keep trying to be like you and like Jesus, your Son, my Savior. Amen.

God Is Omnipresent

Psalm 3:2-6 (MEV): *Many are saying about my life, "There is no help for him in God." Selah. But You, O Lord, are a shield for me, my glory and the One who raises up my head. I cried to the Lord with my voice, and He answered me from His holy hill. Selah. I lay down and slept; I awoke, for the Lord sustained me. I will not be afraid of multitudes of people who have set themselves against me all around.*

Psalm 121:7-8 (MEV): *The Lord shall protect you from all evil; He shall preserve your soul. The Lord shall preserve your going out and your coming in from now and for evermore.*

Jeremiah 29:11-12 (MEV): *For I know the plans that I have for you, says the Lord, plans for peace and not for evil, to give you a future and a hope. Then you shall call upon Me, and you shall come and pray to Me, and I will listen to you.*

Oftentimes, there is a mixture of emotions when someone mistreats or abandoned us. We may feel anger, betrayal, or resentment. When we are going through any trial, it's good not to indulge in negative talking. According to the book of Proverbs, *life and death are in the power of the tongue.* However, there are circumstances that we will go through and will not understand on this side of Heaven. We must depend on God, His Word, and prayer.

ABBA Father, I know you are omnipresent, so you know what I am in need of. Whatever darkness, compromise, or ungodly thing that still exists in my life, no matter how small, today, I root it out. There is no middle ground.

Father, help me to grow in confidence as your child. I bring every part of my life under your covering. Please reveal yourself to those among my family and friends who are still a long way off. Amen.

Can You Hear Me Now?

Psalm 85:8 (MEV): *I will hear what God the Lord will speak, for He will speak peace to His people and to His saints but let them not turn again to folly.*

1 John 5:14-15 (MEV): *This is the confidence that we have in Him, that if we ask anything according to His will, He hears us. So if we know that He hears whatever we ask, we know that we have whatever we asked of Him.*

Revelation 3:20-22 (MEV): *Listen! I stand at the door and knock. If anyone hears My voice and opens the door, I will come in and dine with him, and he with Me. "To him who overcomes will I grant to sit with Me on My throne, as I also overcame and sat down with My Father on His throne. He who has an ear, let him hear what the Spirit says to the churches."*

Don't we all respond better to a person who takes an interest in us and expresses affection versus someone who tries to force or manipulate us to comply with their wishes? Oftentimes, we need someone to practice attentive listening which entails an eagerness to hear everything about our thoughts, feelings, and experiences.

Another suggestion to earning someone's trust is to make full eye contact and do not interrupt or prematurely formulate an answer. Careful listening will encourage someone to bare their soul and share their innermost thoughts and life circumstances. However, we must show a lot of patience and not be anxious for immediate results.

ABBA Father, today I practice dealing with every sin and temptation in its seed form. I throw it out.

Father, please help me to have a willing heart whenever I am called upon to give to others. Help me to demonstrate your love by the things I do. Help me to weigh the words I speak. Help me not to jump to conclusions or hastily voice opinions that are not grounded. Help me to shine your light.

Thank you for those in my life that give wise counsel. Amen.

Words of Encouragement

Romans 15:4-6 (ESV): *For whatever was written in former days was written for our instruction, that through endurance and through the encouragement of the Scriptures we might have hope. May the God of endurance and encouragement grant you to live in such harmony with one another, in accord with Christ Jesus, that together you may with one voice glorify the God and Father of our Lord Jesus Christ.*

1 Thessalonians 5:9-11 (ESV): *For God has not destined us for wrath, but to obtain salvation through our Lord Jesus Christ, who died for us so that whether we are awake or asleep we might live with him. Therefore encourage one another and build one another up, just as you are doing.*

Hebrews 6:17-18 (ESV): *So when God desired to show more convincingly to the heirs of the promise the unchangeable character of his purpose, he guaranteed it with an oath, so that by two unchangeable things, in which it is impossible for God to lie, we who have fled for refuge might have strong encouragement to hold fast to the hope set before us.*

Uplifting words give life. Our loved ones should be the constant recipient of encouragement. This encouragement can come in many forms and for many reasons.

Write a note, send a text, or encourage them in front of someone else. Also, we can point out their personality traits and unique talents that we appreciate. Do not let a day go by without communicating encouraging thoughts to your loved ones.

ABBA Father, help me to only say good things to edify my loved ones and others. Today, in full confidence of the power given me, I overcame.

Jesus, you are the light of the world; shine on me. Let your light penetrates and changes me, helping me to reflect your glory. May I be a light that leads others to you. Amen.

Share Love

1 Thessalonians 3:11-13 (ESV): *Now may our God and Father himself, and our Lord Jesus, direct our way to you, and may the Lord make you increase and abound in love for one another and for all, as we do for you, so that he may establish your hearts blameless in holiness before our God and Father, at the coming of our Lord Jesus with all his saints.*

Hebrews 13:1-3 (ESV): *Let brotherly love continue. Do not neglect to show hospitality to strangers, for thereby some have entertained angels unawares. Remember those who are in prison, as though in prison with them, and those who are mistreated, since you also are in the body.*

1 John 3:17-18 (ESV): *But if anyone has the world's goods and sees his brother in need, yet closes his heart against him, how does God's love abide in him? Little children, let us not love in word or talk but in deed and in truth.*

Discipline, correction, and training are ineffective when void of tender love. These same tools are welcomed more readily if they come with a kind and gentle hand. Make it a point to discover your loved ones' interests and hobbies. Talk about them and learn to share in their enthusiasm or go a step further and participate with them in those activities. Taking an interest need not require financial expense, but it does call for a heart of love and commitment for the things your loved ones enjoy.

ABBA Father, thank you for the perfect example of how to share my love. I make it my aim today to let love, blessings, and joy overflow from me.

Father, you are the Good Shepherd. Thank you for watching over me day and night and for bringing me back when I have strayed.

Please bless our children, grandchildren, and our family members who seem far from you right now. May they hear your voice and come back to you. Amen.

Be A Blessing

Deuteronomy 15:5-7: *If only you fully obey the Lord your God and are careful to follow all these commands I am giving you today. For the Lord, your God will bless you as he has promised, and you will lend to many nations but will borrow from none. You will rule over many nations but none will rule over you. If anyone is poor among your fellow Israelites in any of the towns of the land the Lord your God is giving you, do not be hardhearted or tightfisted toward them.*

Luke 6:37-38 (MEV): *Judge not, and you shall not be judged. Condemn not, and you will not be condemned. Forgive, and you shall be forgiven. Give, and it will be given to you: Good measure, pressed down, shaken together, and running over will men give unto you. For with the measure you use, it will be measured unto you.*

2 Corinthians 9:8-11: *And God is able to bless you abundantly, so that in all things at all times, having all that you need, you will abound in every good work. As it is written: "They have freely scattered their gifts to the poor; their righteousness endures forever." Now he who supplies seed to the sower and bread for food will also supply and increase your store of seed and will enlarge the harvest of your righteousness. You will be enriched in every way so that you can be generous on every occasion, and through us your generosity will result in thanksgiving to God.*

We should always show genuine affection to the ones we love. We can do this verbally by simply saying, *I love you*, many times a day or express physical affection through hugs and kisses.

Another way to express tender love is to plan special outings and find unique ways to make memories. Even throwing in a surprise or two because everybody loves a surprise. Just being kind and affectionate to our loved ones will cause them to want to spend time with us.

ABBA Father, help me to pour out warm kindness and affection to my loved ones and others. Whoever I need to bless, help me to be a blessing to them today.

Father, as you have blessed me, I humble myself to become a blessing to others. Amen.

God Created You For A Purpose

Job 42:1-3: *Then Job replied to the LORD: I know that you can do all things; no purpose of yours can be thwarted. You asked, 'Who is this that obscures my plans without knowledge?' Surely I spoke of things I did not understand, things too wonderful for me to know.*

Proverbs 19:21: *Many are the plans in a person's heart, but it is the Lord's purpose that prevails.*

Romans 8:28: *And we know that in all things God works for the good of those who love him, who have been called according to his purpose.*

There will be ruthless people who cause disrupting confrontations throughout our lives. Our feelings should not decide our focus. If we focus on how someone else feels about us, then we may feel less than them. People only have control over us if we let them and there should be only two viewpoints about our self that matters – God's and yours.

God's viewpoint is that we are fearfully and wonderfully made for a purpose. Finding our purpose is the journey and true joy of life. We must stay the course and see where the journey is going.

ABBA Father, I'm thankful that you desire to speak through me. Help me to learn to depend completely on you and to trust you for the right words at the right time. Whenever I am in a tight spot, I know that you are with me then, giving me just the right words to say to bring your life, light, and hope to people surrounded by darkness. I will give you all the glory because you are the only one who can do this.

Thank you for your wisdom and timing, which are always perfect. Thank you for saving me, loving me, and touching my life. Thank you for creating me for your purpose and for helping me to successfully fulfill it. I use my life to do the same for others. I begin today. Amen.

God Equipped Me For My Assignment

Matthew 28:18-20 (MEV): *Then Jesus came and spoke to them, saying, "All authority has been given to Me in heaven and on earth. Go therefore and make disciples of all nations, baptizing them in the name of the Father and of the Son and of the Holy Spirit, teaching them to observe all things I have commanded you. And remember, I am with you always, even to the end of the age." Amen.*

Mark 16:15-16 (MEV): *He said to them, Go into all the world, and preach the Gospel to every creature. He who believes and is baptized will be saved. But he who does not believe will be condemned.*

Romans 10:14-15 (MEV): *How then shall they call on Him in whom they have not believed? And how shall they believe in Him of whom they have not heard? And how shall they hear without a preacher? And how shall they preach unless they are sent? As it is written: "How beautiful are the feet of those who preach the Gospel of peace, who bring good news of good things!"*

We, as believers in Jesus Christ, all have an inner strength that most people do not have. A strength that can get us through any hurt by having faith in God.

Sharing that faith and the Good News of Jesus Christ is a chosen assignment we all can participate in. This is the chance to be a positive influence over people's destiny.

DEVOTIONAL

ABBA Father, today, even in the most unlikely or lowest of circumstances, I set up my portable mountaintop and dwell with you on the heights.

I am a believer and not a doubter. I hold fast to my confession of faith. I decide to walk by faith and practice faith. My faith comes by hearing Your Word. Jesus is the author and developer of my faith. I choose to spread the Good News of Jesus Christ. Amen.

All My Children

Psalm 127:3-4 (MEV): *Look, children are a gift of the Lord, and the fruit of the womb is a reward. As arrows in the hand of a mighty warrior, so are the children of one's youth.*

Proverbs 22:6 (MEV): *Train up a child in the way he should go, and when he is old he will not depart from it.*

Isaiah 54:13 (MEV): *All your sons shall be taught of the Lord, and great shall be the peace of your sons.*

The Bible instructs parents not to provoke their children to anger. Parents have a powerful influence over their children which can be used for good or evil.

Regardless of the influence we received from our parents, every child grows up and makes his or her own choices in life. Therefore, we as Christian parents must daily pray that our children seek God for guidance and wisdom to fulfill their God-ordained purpose in life.

ABBA Father, I know all children are a gift from you. Father, help me to surrender my children to you and not worry about them. Father, help me to be aware of those moments when I am not willing to be patient. Thank you for being so patient with me.

Father, we thank you that you created them with a specific plan and purpose for their lives. Thank you that they are valuable and precious in your sight.

Father, give them the mind of Christ that is theirs in you and help them to fully know and love who they are in you and this great plan you have for them. Amen.

Seeking God

1 Chronicles 16:10-11 (MEV): *Glory in His holy name; let the heart of those who seek the Lord rejoice. Seek the Lord and His strength; seek His face continually.*

Jeremiah 29:12-13 (MEV): *Then you shall call upon Me, and you shall come and pray to Me, and I will listen to you. You shall seek Me and find Me when you shall search for Me with all your heart.*

Luke 11:9-10 (MEV): *And I tell you, ask, and it will be given to you; seek, and you will find; knock, and it will be opened to you. For everyone who asks receives, and he who seeks finds, and to him who knocks it will be opened.*

Remember that the greatest achievements begin as thoughts. However, we as believers in Jesus Christ must be modest and devout. We must also be careful not to grasp the power and glory that belongs to God.

Jesus commissioned all believers to lead others away from idolatry and back to God. Let us look to God for our strength, strategy, and stamina.

ABBA Father, my greatest fulfillment in life is to know and love you. I make it my aim to receive your love, with no reason or cause, and love others the same way. Please help me to show others how to know and love you.

Father, develop in me a deep reverence of you that leads to life, wisdom, and greater intimacy with you. May I be so filled with your love that faith would replace fear. Amen.

Step By Step, Day By Day

2 Corinthians 5:16-19 (CEV): *We are careful not to judge people by what they seem to be, though we once judged Christ in that way. Anyone who belongs to Christ is a new person. The past is forgotten, and everything is new. God has done it all! He sent Christ to make peace between himself and us, and he has given us the work of making peace between himself and others. What we mean is that God was in Christ, offering peace and forgiveness to the people of this world. And he has given us the work of sharing his message about peace.*

Philippians 2:1-5 (CEV): *Christ encourages you, and his love comforts you. God's Spirit unites you, and you are concerned for others. Now make me completely happy! Live in harmony by showing love for each other. Be united in what you think, as if you were only one person. Don't be jealous or proud but be humble and consider others more important than yourselves. Care about them as much as you care about yourselves and think the same way that Christ Jesus thought.*

2 Timothy 2:1-6 (CEV): *First of all, I ask you to pray for everyone. Ask God to help and bless them all and tell God how thankful you are for each of them. Pray for kings and others in power, so that we may live quiet and peaceful lives as we worship and honor God. This kind of prayer is good, and it pleases God our Savior. God wants everyone to be saved and to know the whole truth, which is, There is only one God, and Christ Jesus is the only one who can bring us to God. Jesus was truly human, and he gave himself to rescue all of us. God showed us this at the right time.*

Oftentimes, we carry the burdens of someone's actions as our fault. We make the choice to love someone with our whole heart. We give our self and that love and trust are thrown away. We must not let this event destroy our future and destiny.

Choose the perspective with which you define life events. Believe that everything can and will work in your favor. With God, we can continue to take life's journey step-by-step, day-by-day, and the healing will come.

ABBA Father, help me to trust in you with all my heart today. Guard me against depending on my own limited understanding. Instead, help me to rely totally on you. I desire to seek your will in all I do today.

Thank you for the promise that you will direct my paths so that I can walk hand in hand with you, depend on your higher understanding, and seek your will in all I do. I am grateful that you are the potter and I am the clay.

Father, help me to trust you as I am molded and made whole again. I believe in your power to bring into existence that which is not. I live this day in that power. I speak that which is not as if it was. Amen.

Forgiveness Heals

Matthew 6:14-15 (MSG): *In prayer there is a connection between what God does and what you do. You can't get forgiveness from God, for instance, without also forgiving others. If you refuse to do your part, you cut yourself off from God's part.*

Mark 11:24-25 (ERV): *So I tell you to ask for what you want in prayer. And if you believe that you have received those things, then they will be yours. When you are praying and you remember that you are angry with another person about something, forgive that person. Forgive them so that your Father in heaven will also forgive your sins.*

Ephesians 4:31-32 (ERV): *Never be bitter, angry, or mad. Never shout angrily or say things to hurt others. Never do anything evil. Be kind and loving to each other. Forgive each other the same as God forgave you through Christ.*

We all need forgiveness in our lives. Forgiveness is an important part of healing. Forgiving someone who has caused heartaches, disappointments, and hard times does not mean you agree with what they have done. It simply means that through forgiveness you cut the ropes that keep you tied to the injury that was brought into your life.

When we forgive, we can start living for the now! None of us can change our yesterdays because they are behind us. None of us can live in our tomorrows because tomorrow may never come. We must never allow our past to determine our future.

ABBA Father, today help me to have a forgiving heart to those who have wronged me. I need to learn how to receive your forgiveness and how to forgive those who have wronged me. I don't want to cause your presence in my life to be quenched because of unforgiveness.

Father, help me to forgive others when what they do annoy me. Help me to forgive myself when I also do irritating things. Create in me a free and forgiving spirit that sees others as you do, responds to them with your heart, and prays for them with your love.

I give thanks to all those things that brought me to you, even the heartaches. Help me to follow the example of Jesus and forgive those who have hurt me. Amen.

God Sees Our Tears

Job 16:19-21: *Even now my witness is in heaven; my advocate is on high. My intercessor is my friend as my eyes pour out tears to God; on behalf of a man he pleads with God as one pleads for a friend.*

Isaiah 38:4-5: *Then the word of the Lord came to Isaiah: Go and tell Hezekiah, This is what the Lord, the God of your father David, says: I have heard your prayer and seen your tears; I will add fifteen years to your life.*

Revelation 21:3-4: *And I heard a loud voice from the throne saying, "Look! God's dwelling place is now among the people, and he will dwell with them. They will be his people, and God himself will be with them and be their God. 'He will wipe every tear from their eyes. There will be no more death' or mourning or crying or pain, for the old order of things has passed away."*

When we are grieving the loss of a loved one or any other tragic event in our lives, we shed many tears. Tears taste salty and salt is to flavor and bless the next experience in our life. We have no seasoning until we cry and take our tears to season the next thing that God serves up in our life.

ABBA Father, I walk in the power of freedom, restoration, reconciliation, and release. I live the power of Jubilee.

Father, thank you for the gifts and talents you have given me. Help me to discover more of what you know I can be so that I can work in your glory. I am grateful that your Word says you will wipe away my tears and give me joy instead. Amen.

Seek Good Counsel

Exodus 18:19-20 (AMPC): *Listen now to [me]; I will counsel you, and God will be with you. You shall represent the people before God, bringing their cases and causes to Him, Teaching them the decrees and laws, showing them the way they must walk and the work they must do.*

Psalm 32:8-9 (AMPC): *I [the Lord] will instruct you and teach you in the way you should go; I will counsel you with My eye upon you. Be not like the horse or the mule, which lack understanding, which must have their mouths held firm with bit and bridle, or else they will not come with you.*

Proverbs 19:20-21 (AMPC): *Hear counsel, receive instruction, and accept correction, that you may be wise in the time to come. Many plans are in a man's mind, but it is the Lord's purpose for him that will stand.*

Christian counseling uses God's Word to counsel others and has nothing to do with psychological counseling. Biblical counseling is used to teach, encourage, rebuke, and guide to help with issues in life.

The counselor with God's wisdom can help unpack the root of depression, anxiety, and fear. Scripture continually tells us to renew our minds. Many times, the cause of our problems is that we stop focusing on Christ and become distracted by everything around us.

We must allow Christ to be our focus. We must set a time every day that we are alone with Him. We must allow God to change our minds and help us think more like Christ.

As Christians, we are to counsel others and listen to wise counsel so we can all grow in Christ. The Holy Spirit, who lives in us, will help us in guidance and learning God's Word. As we pace ourselves through the journey of life, we learn lessons in the valley to help us climb the mountains. Attitude is a frame of mind to conquer our mountains to victory.

ABBA Father, whatever in my life that is broken or a distraction from you, I bring it to Jesus. Father, bless me with a positive attitude to face the circumstances of life that are difficult. Remind me that you are near me and know my good future.

Thank you for your Word in Matthew 18:19-20:

> *Again I say to you, that if two of you agree on earth about anything they ask, it will be done for them by My Father who is in Heaven. For where two or three are assembled in My name, there I am in their midst.*

Amen.

God's Gift Of Children

Psalm 127:3-4 (CEB): *No doubt about it: children are a gift from the Lord; the fruit of the womb is a divine reward. The children born when one is young are like arrows in the hand of a warrior.*

Matthew 18:2-5 (CEB): *Then he called a little child over to sit among the disciples, and said, I assure you that if you don't turn your lives around and become like this little child, you will definitely not enter the kingdom of heaven. Those who humble themselves like this little child will be the greatest in the kingdom of heaven. Whoever welcomes one such child in my name welcomes me.*

Mark 10:13-16 (CEB): *People were bringing children to Jesus so that he would bless them. But the disciples scolded them. When Jesus saw this, he grew angry and said to them, "Allow the children to come to me. Don't forbid them because God's kingdom belongs to people like these children. I assure you that whoever doesn't welcome God's kingdom like a child will never enter it." Then he hugged the children and blessed them.*

We all are made in the image of God, including unborn babies. God places value on every human life. All children have the right to life. God has a purpose and plan for everyone. That plan may be for that unborn child, one day find the cure for a disease or invent something to change the world.

To God, each life is sacred. What sets us apart from all of God's creation is the capability and capacity for love.

ABBA Father, help me to see the value of every human life through your eyes. In Heaven, the good of this life will be retained. I'm thankful that you desire to speak through me.

Father, help me learn how to depend completely on you and to trust you for the right words at the right time. I know that you are especially with me, giving me just the right words to say to bring your life, light, and hope to people surrounded by darkness. I will give you all the glory because you are the only one who can do this.

Thank you for your wisdom and timing, which are always perfect. I do not retain anything of this day that is not good. I retain only what is good. Amen.

History Or Destiny?

Psalm 37:8-9 (MEV): *Let go of anger and forsake wrath; do not fret—it surely leads to evil deeds. For evildoers will be cut off, but those who hope in the Lord will inherit the earth.*

Isaiah 40:30-31 (MEV): *Even the youths shall faint and be weary, and the young men shall utterly fall, but those who wait upon the Lord shall renew their strength; they shall mount up with wings as eagles, they shall run and not be weary, and they shall walk and not faint.*

Jeremiah 29:11-12 (MEV): *For I know the plans that I have for you, says the Lord, plans for peace and not for evil, to give you a future and a hope. Then you shall call upon Me, and you shall come and pray to Me, and I will listen to you.*

We all deserve respect and to be treated with dignity. To be human is to take responsibility for our actions. However, unforgiveness can get so rooted in our inner self that it will choke anything good out. Given enough time our perspective on life can change. Remember where you come from is history and where you are going is destiny.

ABBA Father, you are my shield and my eternal protector. I am so grateful that you are my refuge, my strength, and my ever-present help in trouble. When I am in danger or distress, help me trust in your character. Be my glory and the lifter of my head this day. Lift my gaze and my heart from everything on this earth to you who reign overall.

Thank you for answering me from Heaven and acting on my behalf when I cry out to you. May you be glorified in my life. In you, the best comes at the end. I live this day in full confidence of that fact, looking forward and preparing in hope for that day. Amen.

Choose The Road to Excellence

Philippians 4:7-9 (ESV): *And the peace of God, which surpasses all understanding, will guard your hearts and your minds in Christ Jesus. Finally, brothers, whatever is true, whatever is honorable, whatever is just, whatever is pure, whatever is lovely, whatever is commendable, if there is any excellence, if there is anything worthy of praise, think about these things. What you have learned and received and heard and seen in me—practice these things, and the God of peace will be with you.*

1 Peter 2:9-10 (ESV): *But you are a chosen race, a royal priesthood, a holy nation, a people for his own possession, that you may proclaim the excellencies of him who called you out of darkness into his marvelous light. Once you were not a people, but now you are God's people; once you had not received mercy, but now you have received mercy.*

2 Peter 1:3-4 (ESV): *His divine power has granted to us all things that pertain to life and godliness, through the knowledge of him who called us to his own glory and excellence, by which he has granted to us his precious and very great promises, so that through them you may become partakers of the divine nature, having escaped from the corruption that is in the world because of sinful desire.*

We all make mistakes and some mistakes are engineered and manipulated by other people. We must stop and record the lessons we learn from our mistakes or we are destined to relive them again and again.

We must not be led by our feelings and emotions, which can lead to being prideful and stubborn. Let us choose and pursue goals that will lead to excellence. If you do not know where you are going in life, any road will take you there.

ABBA Father, I am ordinary but you are amazing! You created me and you see things you have placed inside me that I may not recognize yet. When you ask something of me, you also understand what I need to complete the task. Please use me in an excellent way so that people will know that you are behind it all and will exalt your name. I believe and trust in You.

I will be careful to devote myself to pursue goals that are excellent and profitable for everyone. I let the life, the love, the goodness, the power, and the presence of you through my life be born. Amen.

Helpers Of One Another

Zechariah 7:9-12 (ESV): *Thus says the Lord of hosts, Render true judgments, show kindness and mercy to one another, do not oppress the widow, the fatherless, the sojourner, or the poor, and let none of you devise evil against another in your heart. But they refused to pay attention and turned a stubborn shoulder and stopped their ears that they might not hear. They made their hearts diamond-hard lest they should hear the law and the words that the Lord of hosts had sent by his Spirit through the former prophets. Therefore great anger came from the Lord of hosts.*

Matthew 25:35-40 (ESV): *For I was hungry and you gave me food, I was thirsty and you gave me drink, I was a stranger and you welcomed me, I was naked and you clothed me, I was sick and you visited me, I was in prison and you came to me. Then the righteous will answer him, saying, 'Lord, when did we see you hungry and feed you, or thirsty and give you drink? And when did we see you a stranger and welcome you, or naked and clothe you? And when did we see you sick or in prison and visit you?' And the King will answer them, 'Truly, I say to you, as you did it to one of the least of these my brothers, you did it to me.'*

John 13:34-35: *A new command I give you: Love one another. As I have loved you, so you must love one another. By this everyone will know that you are my disciples if you love one another.*

Many non-profit organizations seek volunteers to help women and children escape from sex trafficking and slavery. These non-profits make a difference to women and children who are living through trauma every day. Oftentimes, these women and children do not have anyone to turn to. Therefore, we must show love to those who have been delivered from sex trafficking and slavery.

Through what we do and say others can see the Lord. Is there someone in your life you need to show love to so they can see God's face more clearly? Someone you know might need to hear Him say, *I love you?*

ABBA Father, I do get absorbed sometimes in my own difficulties and I forget to reach out to others who have much greater needs than I do. I ask that you send more laborers to the lost, helpless, and those who are in bondage. I take every need, want, emptiness, desire, or longing and direct it to the Holy Spirit.

I declare mental, physical, and emotional healing for the world in Jesus' Holy Name. Father, help me to trust everything about my life to you. Amen.

Unconditional Love

Psalm 136:1-3: *Give thanks to the Lord, for he is good. His love endures forever. Give thanks to the God of gods. His love endures forever. Give thanks to the Lord of lords: His love endures forever.*

1 Corinthians 13:4-7 (MEV): *Love suffers long and is kind; love envies not; love flaunts not itself and is not puffed up, does not behave itself improperly, seeks not its own, is not easily provoked, thinks no evil; rejoices not in iniquity, but rejoices in the truth; bears all things, believes all things, hopes all things, and endures all things.*

1 John 4:15-16: *If anyone acknowledges that Jesus is the Son of God, God lives in them and they in God. And so we know and rely on the love God has for us. God is love. Whoever lives in love lives in God, and God in them.*

The heart is the inner self that thinks, feels, and makes decisions. The heart is that which is central to a person. The heart symbol represents love and affection for others.

One of the main reasons for time is so all of life does not happen at once. Let us make time and spend it with the ones we love. Kind words are the oil that keeps the friction out of life. Always remember to never underestimate the power of a touch, a smile, a sweet word, a listening ear, an honest compliment, or an act of kindness. Any one of these has the potential to turn a life around.

We should always show genuine affection to the ones we love. We can do this verbally by simply saying, *I love you*, many times a day or express physical affection through hugs and kisses. Just being kind and affectionate to our loved ones will cause them to want to spend time with us.

ABBA Father, I immerse every part of my life in Jesus. Then I walk in the power of freedom, cleansing, restoration, and the breaking of curses.

Father, let me never forget to begin with love in any relationship I have and let my actions speak louder than my words. Thank you for loving me and showing me how to love those close to me. I thank you for loving me unconditionally. I must follow you and love others the same way. Amen.

Two Become One

Genesis 2:22-24 (ESV): *And the rib that the LORD God had taken from the man he made into a woman and brought her to the man. Then the man said, "This at last is bone of my bones and flesh of my flesh; she shall be called Woman, because she was taken out of Man." Therefore a man shall leave his father and his mother and hold fast to his wife, and they shall become one flesh.*

Matthew 19:4-6 (ESV): *He answered, "Have you not read that he who created them from the beginning made them male and female, and said, 'Therefore a man shall leave his father and his mother and hold fast to his wife, and the two shall become one flesh?' So they are no longer two but one flesh. What therefore God has joined together, let not man separate."*

Mark 10:6-9 (ESV): *But from the beginning of creation, 'God made them male and female.' Therefore a man shall leave his father and mother and hold fast to his wife, and the two shall become one flesh.' So they are no longer two but one flesh. What therefore God has joined together, let not man separate.*

Marriage is two separate individuals coming together to make one couple. Becoming one couple does not mean losing your identity as an individual, but working together to accomplish God's purpose in your marriage. With God, a husband and wife are like a three-strand cord intertwined to make one strong rope.

ABBA Father, teach us that marriage is not living for each other. It is two people uniting and joining hands to serve you. Give us a great spiritual purpose in life.

We bring every unanswered question, every unmet need, and every unfulfilled longing to you. May we seek first your kingdom and your righteousness, knowing that you will sustain us through all of life's challenges.

Please help us to learn more about what it means to love each other. Expand our list of ways that we might show love to you and each other. Amen.

Harmonious Marriage

Proverbs 18:22: *He who finds a wife finds what is good and receives favor from the Lord.*

Proverbs 31:10: *A wife of noble character who can find? She is worth far more than rubies.*

Ephesians 5:25-33: *Husbands, love your wives, just as Christ loved the church and gave himself up for her to make her holy, cleansing her by the washing with water through the word, and to present her to himself as a radiant church, without stain or wrinkle or any other blemish, but holy and blameless. In this same way, husbands ought to love their wives as their own bodies. He who loves his wife loves himself. After all, no one ever hated their own body, but they feed and care for their body, just as Christ does the church—for we are members of his body. "For this reason, a man will leave his father and mother and be united to his wife, and the two will become one flesh." This is a profound mystery—but I am talking about Christ and the church. However, each one of you also must love his wife as he loves himself, and the wife must respect her husband.*

Before becoming one as a married couple, pre-marital counseling can help discuss different areas of marriage. Marriage needs to start with no secrets. This world system can be a strain on marriages by having so many issues and distractions.

Oftentimes during the marriage, counseling identifies issues that are important for sustaining and living a successful marriage. Choose a lifestyle of love, faithfulness, caring, sharing, and serving together.

DEVOTIONAL

ABBA Father, I pray for all married and engaged couples to have a loving and devoting marriage together. I pray that they put you, Father, in the center of their marriage so their marriage can evolve around you.

I pray that all couples walk in agreement on the authority of your Word and seek to understand one another. That is more important than being understood. I pray that they will be quick to listen, slow to speak, and slow to anger, in the name of Jesus. Amen.

Peace Of Mind

Isaiah 26:2-4 (ESV): *Open the gates, that the righteous nation that keeps faith may enter in. You keep him in perfect peace whose mind is stayed on you, because he trusts in you. Trust in the Lord forever, for the Lord God is an everlasting rock.*

John 14:26-28 (ESV): *But the Helper, the Holy Spirit, whom the Father will send in my name, he will teach you all things and bring to your remembrance all that I have said to you. Peace I leave with you; my peace I give to you. Not as the world gives do I give to you. Let not your hearts be troubled, neither let them be afraid. You heard me say to you, 'I am going away, and I will come to you.' If you loved me, you would have rejoiced, because I am going to the Father, for the Father is greater than I.*

Philippians 4:5-7: *Let your gentleness be evident to all. The Lord is near. Do not be anxious about anything, but in every situation, by prayer and petition, with thanksgiving, present your requests to God. And the peace of God, which transcends all understanding, will guard your hearts and your minds in Christ Jesus.*

I have learned from past experiences that the real battle of life is in the mind and it is those who are free in their minds are winners and not losers. How we think determines what we say, what we say determines what we have, and what we have determines what we do. When facing hardships, draw strength from God's Word.

ABBA Father, I thank you for your peace which surpasses all understanding. With my soul, I will bless the Lord with every thought and purpose in life. My mind will not wander out of your presence. I set my mind and keep it set on what is above – the higher things – not on the things that are on the earth.

I know that as I follow your leading my story will, in the end, become perfect. Your peace will protect my heart and mind through Christ Jesus. Amen.

Two Ears, One Mouth

Proverbs 12:17-19 (TPT): *Truthfulness marks the righteous, but the habitual liar can never be trusted. Reckless words are like the thrusts of a sword, cutting remarks meant to stab and to hurt. But the words of the wise soothe and heal. Truthful words will stand the test of time, but one day every lie will be seen for what it is.*

Ephesians 4:29 (TPT): *And never let ugly or hateful words come from your mouth, but instead let your words become beautiful gifts that encourage others; do this by speaking words of grace to help them.*

James 1:18-20 (TPT): *God was delighted to give us birth by the truth of his infallible Word so that we would fulfill his chosen destiny for us and become the favorite ones out of all his creation! My dearest brothers and sisters, take this to heart: Be quick to listen, but slow to speak. And be slow to become angry, for human anger is never a legitimate tool to promote God's righteous purpose.*

There are three keys to a successful relationship with family, friends, and co-workers. The first key to a successful relationship is communication. Communication is to talk, converse, and exchange information.

There is a difference between hearing and listening. Hearing is the act or process of perceiving sounds. Listening is making a conscious effort to hear and pay close attention with clear understanding.

ABBA Father, I thank you for two ears to hear more than I speak with my one mouth. I thank you for the wisdom to be able to communicate clearly in all my relationships. I turn from speaking idle words and foolishly talk that are contrary to my true desire to please you. My mouth shall utter truth.

Father, set a guard over my mouth and keep watch over the door of my lips, so I can boldly say that my words are words of faith, power, love, and of life. Then the words of my mouth will produce good things in my life and in the lives of others because I choose your words for my lips and your will for my life. Amen.

Compromise As a Solution

Romans 14:18-19 (ESV): *Whoever thus serves Christ is acceptable to God and approved by men. So then let us pursue what makes for peace and for mutual upbuilding.*

Colossians 3:12-14 (ESV): *Put on then, as God's chosen ones, holy and beloved, compassionate hearts, kindness, humility, meekness, and patience, bearing with one another and, if one has a complaint against another, forgiving each other; as the Lord has forgiven you, so you also must forgive. And above all these put on love, which binds everything together in perfect harmony.*

1 Peter 3:8-11 (ESV): *Finally, all of you, have unity of mind, sympathy, brotherly love, a tender heart, and a humble mind. Do not repay evil for evil or reviling for reviling, but on the contrary, bless, for to this you were called, that you may obtain a blessing. For whoever desires to love life and see good days, let him keep his tongue from evil and his lips from speaking deceit; let him turn away from evil and do good; let him seek peace and pursue it.*

There are three keys to a successful relationship with family, friends, and co-workers. The second key to a successful relationship is compromise. Compromise is to give and take, to yield, and to negotiate when you cannot totally agree.

Oftentimes, relationship issues cannot be agreed on. Before any disagreement becomes intense to the point where hurting words are being said that may not be easily forgiven, you should retreat to determine a compromise. Individually, you should seek God and His Word and then return calmer, clearer, and able to discuss what God has shared with you. When there is an agreement between the two of you, then you have power against the devil and all evil.

Dear Jesus, today I respond to any problem, setback, hindrance, or attack by pressing on more to apprehend the victory that lies just beyond it. Therefore, I take unto myself your whole armor that I may be able to withstand in the evil day. I stand, therefore having my loins girt about with truth. Your Word, Father, which is truth, contains all the weapons of my warfare which are mighty through You to the pulling down of strongholds. Your Word says where two or three are gathered in your name, there you are in our midst. We pray that all compromises lead to harmonious relationships and defeat against our enemies. Amen.

Fully Committed

Galatians 6:9-10 (NLV): *Do not let yourselves get tired of doing good. If we do not give up, we will get what is coming to us at the right time. Because of this, we should do good to everyone. For sure, we should do good to those who belong to Christ.*

Hebrews 10:23-25 (NLV): *Let us hold on to the hope we say we have and not be changed. We can trust God that He will do what He promised. Let us help each other to love others and to do good. Let us not stay away from church meetings. Some people are doing this all the time. Comfort each other as you see the day of His return coming near.*

1 Peter 4:8-10 (NLV): *Most of all, have a true love for each other. Love covers many sins. Be happy to have people stay for the night and eat with you. God has given each of you a gift. Use it to help each other. This will show God's loving-favor.*

There are three keys to a successful relationship with family, friends, and co-workers. The third key to a successful relationship is commitment. Commitment is a promise, pledge, and devotion. Any relationship must include equal giving or equal sacrifice. A commitment in marriage must include love only for each other. Marriage is a daily work to make a life-long commitment.

ABBA Father, I am grateful for being on the receiving end of your love and grace. In all things, today, I look to see your grace. I follow it, act in it, and let everything flow out of it. I am rooted deep in love and founded securely on love, knowing that you are on my side and nothing can separate me from your love. I commit to doing the same in all my relationships. Amen.

No Hide-And-Seek With God

1 Chronicles 16:10-11 (ESV): *Glory in his holy name; let the hearts of those who seek the Lord rejoice! Seek the Lord and his strength; seek his presence continually!*

Jeremiah 29:12-13 (ESV): *Then you will call upon me and come and pray to me, and I will hear you. You will seek me and find me when you seek me with all your heart.*

Hebrews 11:6 (ESV): *And without faith it is impossible to please him, for whoever would draw near to God must believe that he exists and that he rewards those who seek him.*

The Lord is good to them that wait for Him, for the enjoyment of Him is our portion in this world and in that to come. They that wait for the Lord will not be ashamed or disappointed of what they expect. They will renew their spiritual strength and grow stronger and stronger; they will inherit the new heavens and the new earth. They will enjoy many blessings now and have good things laid up for them hereafter.

What we expect we must wait for in faith and hope. Therefore, let us seek the Lord by prayer and supplication early, before, and above all things. We must seek Him earnestly and diligently, with our whole spirit, heart, and soul. God is good to those who are seeking and a rewarder of them in grace with eternal glory and happiness.

ABBA Father, I am so grateful that I do not have to play hide-and-seek with you. When I seek you with all my heart, soul, and mind, I will find you. I live today considering that fact. I cast all my anxieties, worries, concerns for my future, once and for all on you for you care for me affectionately and watchfully.

I expect a life of victory and awesome deeds because my actions are done on behalf of a spirit humbly submitted to your truth and righteousness. Amen.

God Is My Help

Psalm 146:5: *Blessed are those whose help is the God of Jacob; whose hope is in the Lord their God.*

Isaiah 41:10-13: *So do not fear, for I am with you; do not be dismayed, for I am your God. I will strengthen you and help you; I will uphold you with my righteous right hand. All who rage against you will surely be ashamed and disgraced; those who oppose you will be as nothing and perish. Though you search for your enemies, you will not find them. Those who wage war against you will be as nothing at all. For I am the Lord your God who takes hold of your right hand and says to you, Do not fear; I will help you.*

Hebrews 13:6: *So we say with confidence, "The Lord is my helper; I will not be afraid. What can mere mortals do to me?"*

Happy is he that has the God of Heaven and earth for his help. Our happiness indeed is true and the real delight is knowing our Heavenly Father. The God of Jacob is the God of the covenant; He is the only living and true God.

The Lord never dies neither do His thoughts perish. His love and mercy endure throughout all eternity. By resting in the Lord, we know happiness which is beyond description and beyond comparison. A blessed life is to know that God is our present help and our eternal hope. Hallelujah!

ABBA Father, I thank you for being my God of hope. I trust you, your will, and your plans for my life. I join every part of my life to your life and let every part of your life be joined to me. You are the God who cares for us watchfully and hears our prayers, simply because we are your children.

I ask that you show me your unfailing love today in whatever unexpected, wonderful ways you choose. I draw near to you and seek refuge from my enemies. Thank you for hiding me in the shadow of your wings. Thank you for your tender, fatherly care. Amen.

A Brighter Future

2 Samuel 7:18-19: *Then King David went in and sat before the Lord, and he said: Who am I, Sovereign Lord, and what is my family, that you have brought me this far? And as if this were not enough in your sight, Sovereign Lord, you have also spoken about the future of the house of your servant—and this decree, Sovereign Lord, is for a mere human!*

Proverbs 23:17-18: *Do not let your heart envy sinners, but always be zealous for the fear of the Lord. There is surely a future hope for you, and your hope will not be cut off.*

Jeremiah 29:11: *For I know the plans I have for you, declares the Lord, plans to prosper you and not to harm you, plans to give you hope and a future.*

Eventually, the prosperity of the wicked and the afflictions of the righteous comes to an end. Therefore, there is no reason to envy the one nor to be stressed under the other. The reward for the righteous will be peace and prosperity forever.

Our hope is well-founded upon the person and righteousness of Christ, He is our anchor. He is our expectation of grace while in this life and the eternal glory in the world to come. We will enjoy what we are hoping, expecting, and waiting for if we faint not.

ABBA Father, I commit my afflictions into your hands and appoint them for the fulfillment of your purposes. You are the everlasting God; I will put my trust in you alone for your strength is insurmountable and your time is without end. My life is short and my strength is limited, but you promised to be with me in the harshest of circumstances.

Father, I trust in Your promise and rely on your everlasting love. I thank you that I have a brighter future according to your plans. Amen.

Wisdom

Psalm 37:30-31 (NLV): *The mouth of the man who is right with God speaks wisdom. And his tongue speaks what is fair and right. The Law of his God is in his heart. His steps do not leave it.*

Proverbs 3:13-18 (NLV): *Happy is the man who finds wisdom, and the man who gets understanding. For it is better than getting silver and fine gold. She is worth more than stones of great worth. Nothing you can wish for compares with her. Long life is in her right hand. Riches and honor are in her left hand. Her ways are pleasing, and all her paths are peace. She is a tree of life to those who take hold of her. Happy are all who hold her near.*

James 1:5-6 (NLV): *If you do not have wisdom, ask God for it. He is always ready to give it to you and will never say you are wrong for asking. You must have faith as you ask Him. You must not doubt. Anyone who doubts is like a wave which is pushed around by the sea.*

The knowledge of Christ, the Wisdom of God, is the most pleasant and profitable in all the world. When we have found wisdom, there will be a reward in the now and hereafter, for it is the beginning of life eternal.

Oftentimes, there may be some difficulty in the pursuit of wisdom. However, by reading, prayer, and meditation on the Word of God, we can obtain wisdom. They that know wisdom place their hope in Christ. This hope will not be disappointing, their expectations will not disappear, and they will have what is promised unto them.

ABBA Father, I pour out my life like Jesus that I might bless others.

ABBA Father, I believe in you and I like knowing that you rule over my life, that you are in control. Help me to know when you want me to trust in my choices and move forward with confidence. I thank you for your wisdom to make good decisions in every area of my life. Amen.

Help In Times Of Trouble

Psalm 33:20-21: *We wait in hope for the Lord; he is our help and our shield. In him our hearts rejoice, for we trust in his holy name.*

Isaiah 41:10-13: *So do not fear, for I am with you; do not be dismayed, for I am your God. I will strengthen you and help you; I will uphold you with my righteous right hand. All who rage against you will surely be ashamed and disgraced; those who oppose you will be as nothing and perish. Though you search for your enemies, you will not find them. Those who wage war against you will be as nothing at all. For I am the Lord your God who takes hold of your right hand and says to you, Do not fear; I will help you.*

Hebrews 4:15-16: *For we do not have a high priest who is unable to empathize with our weaknesses, but we have one who has been tempted in every way, just as we are—yet he did not sin. Let us then approach God's throne of grace with confidence, so that we may receive mercy and find grace to help us in our time of need.*

The Lord is our help in times of trouble when no one else is or can be. He is a present help and our shield, who surrounds us with His love and favor. The Lord encourages those who are waiting and expecting good things from Him.

From the Word of God, we learn God's joy is essential to our strength. This real joy is heartfelt and inwardly full of glory. God is Holy and so faithful to every Word of His promises, therefore He is to be trusted.

ABBA Father, in the face of whatever evil, trouble, attack, or sin I am dealing with, I don't give in. I do not give up.

Father, I bow down before you, praising and thanking you, acknowledging your devoted and faithful love. Shape me with your love and separate me from everything that keeps me from you. May you be the first and greatest love of my life. I am grateful and thankful for you are my help and I can trust you to rescue me. Amen.

God's Thoughts

Psalm 139:16-18 (ESV): *Your eyes saw my unformed substance; in your book were written, every one of them, the days that were formed for me, when as yet there was none of them. How precious to me are your thoughts, O God! How vast is the sum of them! If I would count them, they are more than the sand. I awake, and I am still with you.*

Isaiah 55:8-9 (ESV): *For my thoughts are not your thoughts, neither are your ways my ways, declares the Lord. For as the heavens are higher than the earth, so are my ways higher than your ways and my thoughts than your thoughts.*

1 Corinthians 2:11-12 (ESV): *For who knows a person's thoughts except the spirit of that person, which is in him? So also no one comprehends the thoughts of God except the Spirit of God. Now we have received not the spirit of the world, but the Spirit who is from God, that we might understand the things freely given us by God.*

God has many thoughts in a way of love, grace, and mercy toward His children. God's thoughts are of peace and not evil or for evil. God's thoughts are to give us an expected and a very desirable end. God's thoughts are to give us a future such as we hoped to have. God's thoughts put an end to all our troubles and put us into the enjoyment of all good things promised.

ABBA Father, I thank you for your strategic plans for my life. I must trust the fact your plans are from a heart of LOVE for me. Today, I make it my goal to give to others the very thing I seek.

Father, teach me what it means to honor you, to call upon, rely upon, and praise your Holy Name. Never let me take your name in vain but help me to remember that I am called to live in a way that glorifies you. Amen.

The Word Doesn't Fail

Isaiah 55:10-11: *As the rain and the snow come down from heaven, and do not return to it without watering the earth and making it bud and flourish, so that it yields seed for the sower and bread for the eater, so is my word that goes out from my mouth: It will not return to me empty, but will accomplish what I desire and achieve the purpose for which I sent it.*

1 Thessalonians 2:13: *And we also thank God continually because, when you received the word of God, which you heard from us, you accepted it not as a human word, but as it actually is, the word of God, which is indeed at work in you who believe.*

2 Timothy 3:16-17: *All Scripture is God-breathed and is useful for teaching, rebuking, correcting and training in righteousness, so that the servant of God may be thoroughly equipped for every good work.*

Those who have a close personal relationship with God are naturally glad when they see and speak with other believers, especially with those whose faith and patience have carried them through troubles and caused them to have victory over trials or temptations.

When we have hope in God's Word, we will not be disappointed. Therefore, the testimony of others presents fresh encouragement to all during their warfare while undergoing similar troubles and temptations. They will be glad when they see in other believers an extraordinary example of the fruit of hoping in God's grace.

DEVOTIONAL

ABBA Father, I am grateful for Your Word which cannot fail. Your Word is more powerful than any trial or temptation that I am experiencing right now. Holy Father, slow to anger, abounding in steadfast love and mercy, yet just and powerful, hear this prayer. Let my cry reach you. You see my misery. You know my hidden sins. Come and rescue me and lead me into freedom. Give me the grace to persevere. Show me the way and I will follow you. Amen.

Labor Of Love

Matthew 22:37-39: *Jesus replied: Love the Lord your God with all your heart and with all your soul and with all your mind. This is the first and greatest commandment. And the second is like it: Love your neighbor as yourself.*

1 Thessalonians 4:8-12: *Therefore, anyone who rejects this instruction does not reject a human being but God, the very God who gives you his Holy Spirit. Now about your love for one another we do not need to write to you, for you yourselves have been taught by God to love each other. And in fact, you do love all of God's family throughout Macedonia. Yet we urge you, brothers and sisters, to do so more and more, and to make it your ambition to lead a quiet life: You should mind your own business and work with your hands, just as we told you, so that your daily life may win the respect of outsiders and so that you will not be dependent on anybody.*

Hebrews 6:10-11: *God is not unjust; he will not forget your work and the love you have shown him as you have helped his people and continue to help them. We want each of you to show this same diligence to the very end, so that what you hope for may be fully realized.*

God is faithful to believers by His own promises in His Word. These promises He was not obligated to make, but once made His righteousness requires Him to keep them. Therefore, whatever God has promised He will certainly fulfill.

God has promised to reward every good work and labor of love. He will surely reward yours. Every good work must spring from faith in the name and goodness of God. Every work that is truly good must have love as its motivation.

ABBA Father, help me to show your love in everything I say and do today. Today, I take time to ponder and take in your love that removed my sins as far as the east is from the west and I will live accordingly.

Father, you created my innermost being; you knit me together in my mother's womb. You know when I sit and when I rise. You perceive my thoughts from afar. Truly, I'm fearfully and wonderfully made. I praise you, ABBA Father. Amen.

Live A Life Of Love

Leviticus 19:18: *Do not seek revenge or bear a grudge against anyone among your people but love your neighbor as yourself. I am the Lord.*

John 13:34-35: *A new command I give you: Love one another. As I have loved you, so you must love one another. By this everyone will know that you are my disciples if you love one another.*

1 John 4:7-8: *Dear friends, let us love one another, for love comes from God. Everyone who loves has been born of God and knows God. Whoever does not love does not know God, because God is love.*

By faith, we receive spiritual blessings and walk with God. It is impossible to please God without faith. By hope, we expect a future and pass through things temporal so as not to lose those which are eternal. By love, we resemble God and show forth this love in living a life of obedience to God and compassion and helpfulness to the world.

Father, thank you for loving me and help me to show your love to this world. Today, I draw near to you in worship, in love, in joy, in the deepest of intimacy. I have learned that you are the peace I seek. No one else can give me what I long for. Fill me with your presence and give me a heart of peace. Amen.

Christ Is My Anchor

Job 11:17-18: *Life will be brighter than noonday, and darkness will become like morning. You will be secure, because there is hope; you will look about you and take your rest in safety.*

Isaiah 26:3-4: *You will keep in perfect peace those whose minds are steadfast, because they trust in you. Trust in the Lord forever, for the Lord, the Lord himself, is the Rock eternal.*

Hebrews 6:19-20: *We have this hope as an anchor for the soul, firm and secure. It enters the inner sanctuary behind the curtain, where our forerunner, Jesus, has entered on our behalf. He has become a high priest forever, in the order of Melchizedek.*

This world is as a sea; the church and every believer are in it as a ship. The port of call is Heaven; Christ is the pilot and Hope is the anchor. An anchor is launched to the bottom of the sea and is out of sight. When the ship is in a calm, in danger of a rock, or near the shore, the anchor keeps the ship steady. However, when the ship is at anchor it does not move forward.

An anchor is not of any use in a tempest, but hope is with the soul. The anchor of hope without the cable of faith is of little service, but being anchored in Christ keeps the soul steady and secured. When the anchor of hope is in motion it is directed onto Christ because He is our ground and foundation.

DEVOTIONAL

Dear Jesus, forgive me for the times that I have only paid lip service to your lordship in my life. I have prayed one thing and done another. Help me, as of this moment, to experience the joy of serving you and living with the knowledge that you are my anchor. I am grateful that I can depend on you to be my anchor as I go through the storms of life. Amen.

No Expiration Date

Joshua 21:44-45: *The Lord gave them rest on every side, just as he had sworn to their ancestors. Not one of their enemies withstood them; the Lord gave all their enemies into their hands. Not one of all the Lord's good promises to Israel failed; everyone was fulfilled.*

1 Kings 8:55-57: *He stood and blessed the whole assembly of Israel in a loud voice, saying: Praise be to the Lord, who has given rest to his people Israel just as he promised. Not one word has failed of all the good promises he gave through his servant Moses. May the Lord our God be with us as he was with our ancestors; may he never leave us nor forsake us.*

Hebrews 10:23: *Let us hold unswervingly to the hope we profess, for he who promised is faithful.*

Now God is faithful to all His promises. He is all-wise and foreknowing of everything that will come to pass. God never forgets His Word and He can perform it. He is the only God of truth and He cannot lie, nor has He ever failed in any of His promises, nor will His faithfulness fail. Let us live by our declaration of faith without wavering.

ABBA Father, what barriers are hindering me and your will in my life? Please identify them and then, by your power, I can cross over them.

Thank you for your promises to be with me and, if I stray, please call me back. Increase and deepen my confidence that you are near. I declare today to have faith in you because without faith it's impossible to please you. Amen.

New Mercies Every Day

1 Kings 8:22-24 (MEV): *Then Solomon stood in front of the altar of the Lord in the presence of all the congregation of Israel and spread his hands toward heaven. And he said, Lord God of Israel, there is no God like You in heaven above or on earth below who keeps covenant and mercy with Your servants who walk before You with all their hearts, who have kept what You promised Your servant David my father. You spoke also with Your mouth and have fulfilled it with Your hand, as it is this day.*

Psalm 106:1 (MEV): *Praise the Lord! Oh, give thanks unto the Lord, for He is good, for His mercy endures forever.*

Lamentations 3:22-23 (MEV): *It is of the Lord's mercies that we are not consumed; His compassions do not fail. They are new every morning; great is Your faithfulness.*

Our God is "The God of Hope" and we should hope in Him only. God has great things in store for His people, for with the Lord there is mercy.

Mercy has been shown to us, but it dwells in God. It is one of His perfections. There is mercy with the Lord in all its tenderness. God is full of compassion and His tender mercies are over us.

ABBA Father, I pray for justice for all who are oppressed, particularly for those who are poor, infirm, or helpless. I pray for women and children throughout the world. Protect and defend them, bringing their oppressors speedily to justice. Let the whole world rejoice in your justice. I thank you for new mercies every day. Amen.

Wait On The Lord

Psalm 130:5: *I wait for the LORD, my whole being waits, and in His Word, I put my hope.*

Isaiah 40:30-31 (MEV): *Even the youths shall faint and be weary, and the young men shall utterly fall, but those who wait upon the Lord shall renew their strength; they shall mount up with wings as eagles, they shall run and not be weary, and they shall walk and not faint.*

Lamentations 3:25-26 (MEV): *The Lord is good to those who wait for Him, to the soul who seeks Him. It is good that a man should wait quietly for the salvation of the Lord.*

I wait for the Lord, expecting Him to come to me in love. He is worth waiting for.

Waiting is a part of life's discipline and it is a posture of faith. It gives time for preparation for the coming gift. It makes the blessing that much sweeter when it arrives. Oh, have faith in God.

Waiting is also a prayerful and patient posture. There is not a more God-honoring grace of the Christian character than patience. Waiting is the posture of rest. When we wait for the Lord, we are resting in the Lord. In all your waiting remember two things: 1) Let it not be so much the event which you wait for as your focus, 2) but the Lord in the event as your main focus.

ABBA Father, help me to patiently wait. You don't operate on my time schedule but on your grace schedule. I ponder the grace that brought me from far away into your Kingdom. And, if I can, I will help bring near those still far away.

I bless your name, **ABBA** Father, the one who sees my needs and provides for them. Hallowed be thy name! Amen.

A Word Of Promise

Romans 4:20-21 (MEV): *He did not waver at the promise of God through unbelief, but was strong in faith, giving glory to God, and being fully persuaded that what God had promised, He was able to perform.*

2 Corinthians 1:18-20 (MEV): *But as God is true, we did not tell you "Yes" and "No." For the Son of God, Jesus Christ, who was preached among you by us, even by Silas, Timothy, and me, was not "Yes" and "No." In Him it was "Yes." For all the promises of God in Him are "Yes," and in Him "Amen," to the glory of God through us.*

Hebrews 10:35-37 (MEV): *Therefore do not throw away your confidence, which will be greatly rewarded. For you need patience, so that after you have done the will of God, you will receive the promise. For, In yet a little while, He who is to come will come, and will not wait.*

God can never forget His promise or be unconscious of His Word. However, when unbelief exits, doubts emerge, and faith is not active in us, it seems God has delayed the accomplishment of His promise.

A word of promise is a good ground of hope, and the hope which is applied on the promise is not of a man's self, it is the gift of God. King David had his afflictions, and so has everyone; none are without. Therefore, the Word of God is our comfort under them; the written Word, heard or read, and especially a word of promise.

ABBA Father, today I take my eyes off my circumstances and focus only on my destination. I press on to the good, the highest, and the Heavenly.

Jesus, you are the great physician, the one who can heal both body and soul. Come today with your great mercy and your wonderful healing power. I surrender my doubts as I wait for the manifestation of all your promises. Amen.

The Peace Maker

Isaiah 9:6-7: *For to us a child is born, to us a son is given, and the government will be on his shoulders. And he will be called Wonderful Counselor, Mighty God, Ever-lasting Father, Prince of Peace. Of the greatness of his government and peace there will be no end. He will reign on David's throne and over his kingdom, establishing and upholding it with justice and righteousness from that time on and forever. The zeal of the Lord Almighty will accomplish this.*

Romans 5:1-2: *Therefore, since we have been justified through faith, we have peace with God through our Lord Jesus Christ, through whom we have gained access by faith into this grace in which we now stand. And we boast in the hope of the glory of God.*

Colossians 3:15: *Let the peace of Christ rule in your hearts, since as members of one body you were called to peace. And be thankful.*

One of the precious benefits and privileges which flow from justification is peace with God. By faith, we lay hold of God's arm and, by His strength, we are at peace. In this peace with God, there is friendship and loving-kindness. This is through our Lord Jesus Christ —through Him as the great Peacemaker, the Mediator between God and mankind.

Dear Jesus, forgive me for the times when my heart and mind are not fixed upon you and I lack your peace. When fear comes and peace is wanting, help me to come quickly to you who satisfies me and gives me purpose.

Your peace passes all my understanding. I cease from all straying and draw near to you my shepherd. I rest in the protection and the tender love of your arms. I praise you for the peace you have given me through the cross. Thank you for being the Prince of Peace. Amen.

Overflow With Hope

Psalm 33:21-22: *In him our hearts rejoice, for we trust in his holy name. May your unfailing love be with us, Lord, even as we put our hope in you.*

Romans 15:13: *May the God of hope fill you with all joy and peace as you trust in Him, so that you may overflow with hope by the power of the Holy Spirit.*

1 Timothy 6:17: *Command those who are rich in this present world not to be arrogant nor to put their hope in wealth, which is so uncertain, but to put their hope in God, who richly provides us with everything for our enjoyment.*

Romans 15:13 is a wonderful prayer that the Apostle Paul wants every believer to experience. When you read a verse like this, you must ask yourself:

- Does this verse even come close to describing me?
- Can I honestly say that my life is filled with all joy and peace?
- Do I even have hope?

We all want and need these qualities and, yet, even among believers, very few can claim to have joy, peace, and hope. A common factor among those who are depressed is that they lack hope. Discouraged people and those who are unmotivated about life also lack hope.

However, if we lack hope, the first place we should look for it is in God, who is the source of true hope. Ask God to fill you to the overflow with His joy, peace, and hope. God's loving kindnesses indeed never cease, for His compassions never fail. His mercies are new every morning and great is His faithfulness.

ABBA Father, I take all the regrets, shame, and guilt that I have ever carried in my life and give them to Jesus. I let them go forever. I am determined to be more aware of you in every aspect of my life. Great is your faithfulness every day.

Father, I need an overflow of joy, peace, and hope that only you can give to sustain me through life's journey. Amen.

The Love Of God Has No Limits

Psalm 136:1-3: *Give thanks to the Lord, for he is good. His love endures forever. Give thanks to the God of gods. His love endures forever. Give thanks to the Lord of lords: His love endures forever.*

Romans 8:37-39: *No, in all these things we are more than conquerors through him who loved us. For I am convinced that neither death nor life, neither angels nor demons, neither the present nor the future, nor any powers, neither height nor depth, nor anything else in all creation, will be able to separate us from the love of God that is in Christ Jesus our Lord.*

John 3:16-17: *For God so loved the world that he gave his one and only Son, that whoever believes in him shall not perish but have eternal life. For God did not send his Son into the world to condemn the world, but to save the world through him.*

The love of God can never depend upon anything that we can do. The love of God is plentiful and more abundant than we can ever imagine. Now the love which the Spirit deposits deeply in the heart as all the fruit of peace with God, access to the throne of grace and we can rejoice in hope of the glory of God.

Dear Jesus, I meditate on the fact that you are my covering for every moment of my life – always and forever. I live accordingly.

Father, I am so grateful that you are the epitome of love. Help me to feel your love each day and, when I don't, help me to know for sure that it is still there. Your Word says that absolutely nothing can separate me from your love. Thank you. Amen.

Faith Is Essential

Matthew 21:21-22 (MEV): *Jesus answered them, "Truly I say to you, if you have faith and do not doubt, you will not only do what was done to the fig tree, but also, if you say to this mountain, 'Be removed, and be thrown into the sea,' it will be done. And whatever you ask in prayer, if you believe, you will receive."*

Romans 1:16-17 (MEV): *For I am not ashamed of the Gospel of Christ. For it is the power of God for salvation to everyone who believes, to the Jew first, and also to the Greek. For in it the righteousness of God is revealed from faith to faith. As it is written, "The just shall live by faith."*

Hebrews 11:1 (MEV): *Now faith is the substance of things hoped for, the evidence of things not seen.*

Faith is a solid certainty of the power, faithfulness, love, and all special blessings of God. Faith is the essential foundation of hope. Faith is having an expectation of things yet not enjoyed, difficult to be obtained, though possible through Christ. Therefore, without Faith, there would be no hope of which is promised. Faith is a future yet to come with Christ and eternal glory.

ABBA Father, what in my life is still incomplete? Instead of trying to fill it, I find my completion in you and let your fullness fill what is empty.

Father, thank you for giving me so many ways to connect with you and to understand you. Thank you for guiding me through your love, your Word, and your Holy Spirit.

Thank you for my measure of faith which gives me hope to trust in your Word. Amen.

Love One Another

John 13:34-35: *A new command I give you: Love one another. As I have loved you, so you must love one another. By this everyone will know that you are my disciples if you love one another.*

1 Corinthians 13:4-8: *Love is patient, love is kind. It does not envy, it does not boast, it is not proud. It does not dishonor others, it is not self-seeking, it is not easily angered, it keeps no record of wrongs. Love does not delight in evil but rejoices with the truth. It always protects, always trusts, always hopes, always perseveres. Love never fails.*

1 John 4:7-8: *Dear friends, let us love one another, for love comes from God. Everyone who loves has been born of God and knows God. Whoever does not love does not know God, because God is love.*

We must not envy the momentary happiness of those who are doing wrong. When we show love to God, Christ, and mankind, we are obeying the greatest commandments. Therefore, when showing love, it's not to run carelessly into promoting one's own honor and interests without considering what will be the consequence of our actions.

Oftentimes, we can be reckless with the words that proceed from our mouth which can be unacceptable before God and man. Words are like toothpaste: once it's out of the tube, there's no putting it back in. Love shows wisdom and knowledge with grace to one another.

ABBA Father, I live this day seeking to follow your will and purposes and to bear witness of your existence in everything I do. Jesus, thank you for your friendship, for delivering me, and for hearing my prayers. Thank you for linking me together with so many of your friends throughout the world. Because of you, I am not alone. I thank you for the perfect example of Jesus to show me how to love. Amen.

The Lord's Mercies

Deuteronomy 4:30-31 (MEV): *When you are in distress and all these things come upon you, even in the latter days, if you turn to the Lord your God and shall be obedient to His voice (for the Lord your God is a merciful God), He will not abandon you or destroy you or forget the covenant of your fathers which He swore to them.*

Lamentations 3:20-22 (MEV): *Surely my soul remembers and is humbled within me. But this I call to mind, and therefore I have hope: It is of the Lord's mercies that we are not consumed; His compassions do not fail.*

Hebrews 4:15-16 (MEV): *For we do not have a High Priest who cannot sympathize with our weaknesses, but One who was in every sense tempted like we are, yet without sin. Let us then come with confidence to the throne of grace, that we may obtain mercy and find grace to help in time of need.*

We can have confidence, faith, and hope that God will in His mercy remember us and our trials and temptations and save us. There is an abundance of mercy, grace, and goodness in God. In His Word are numerous occurrences of His blessings because His compassions never fail. God's mercies are from everlasting to everlasting.

ABBA Father, I live this day as one who has been chosen to be a part of your Kingdom. I'm a spirit learning to live in a natural world. I have a soul and I live in a physical body. I'm in the world, but I am not of the world.

Thank you for your Spirit who guides me into all truth. I thank you because your love and faithfulness never cease, I have new mercies every day. Amen.

Stay On Guard

Proverbs 4:21-23 (NCV): *Don't ever forget my words; keep them always in mind. They are the key to life for those who find them; they bring health to the whole body. Be careful what you think because your thoughts run your life.*

Isaiah 26:3-4 (MEV): *You will keep him in perfect peace, whose mind is stayed on You, because he trusts in You. Trust in the Lord forever, for in God the Lord we have an everlasting rock.*

1 Peter 1:13 (MEV): *Therefore, guard your minds, be sober, and hope to the end for the grace that is to be brought to you at the revelation of Jesus Christ.*

We as believers must guard our minds and thoughts against the cares of this life. Let us run the race as believers toward the Heavenly Kingdom.

Stay prepared and ready to do every good work at the assignment you are given. Serve Jesus Christ with joy and without grumbling in whatsoever He called you to. Wait patiently and with expectation for His coming.

It is by grace that we continually rejoice and come to the enjoyment of what we are hoping for, believing and trusting to that eternal glory and happiness. Grace is the gift of God through Christ to His children.

ABBA Father, I realize there is a battlefield in my mind to stay focused on what is pleasing to you and to have your peace. I choose the Word over the world, over my circumstances, my problems, and everything else.

Jesus, help me to stop making excuses for myself. Whenever I begin to do this, interrupt my thoughts, and remind me of your Word. Amen.

Hope Is In The Bible

2 Samuel 22:31-32: *As for God, his way is perfect: The Lord's word is flawless; he shields all who take refuge in him. For who is God besides the Lord? And who is the Rock except our God?*

Romans 15:4 (MEV): *For whatever was previously written was written for our instruction, so that through perseverance and encouragement of the Scriptures we might have hope.*

2 Timothy 3:16-17 (MEV): *All Scripture is inspired by God and is profitable for teaching, for reproof, for correction, and for instruction in righteousness, that the man of God may be complete, thoroughly equipped for every good work.*

The sacred scriptures of the Bible are to inform us of how we ought to behave both towards God and men. The scriptures are not only written for our present instruction, but for encouraging and establishing a hope of eternal life.

The Bible was given by divine grace to give us a clear account of the great and precious promises secured in Christ. The Bible gives an account of the true nature of patience in bearing all sorts of evils. The Bible informs us of the best principles to maintain hope during our journey through life.

ABBA Father, the incorruptible seed, the living Word, the Word of truth is abiding in my spirit. That seed is growing mightily in me now, producing your nature and your life. It is my counsel, shield, buckler, and powerful weapon in battle.

The Word is a lamp to my feet and a light to my path. It makes my way plain before me. I do not stumble for my steps are ordered in the Word. I ask for clarity and wisdom when I read your Holy Word.

Father, help me to apply your Word to every area of my life. Amen.

Faith Walk

Romans 3:21-23 (NLV): *But now God has made another way to make men right with Himself. It is not by the Law. The Law and the early preachers tell about it. Men become right with God by putting their trust in Jesus Christ. God will accept men if they come this way. All men are the same to God. For all men have sinned and have missed the shining-greatness of God.*

Galatians 3:25-27 (NLV): *Now that our faith is in Christ, we do not need the Law to lead us. You are now children of God because you have put your trust in Christ Jesus. All of you who have been baptized to show you belong to Christ have become like Christ.*

Colossians 1:22-23 (NLV): *But Christ has brought you back to God by His death on the cross. In this way, Christ can bring you to God, holy and pure and without blame. This is for you if you keep the faith. You must not change from what you believe now. You must not leave the hope of the Good News you received. The Good News was preached to you and to all the world. And I, Paul, am one of Christ's missionaries.*

When we persevere in faith then we can hold on through all the circumstances of life to the end. However, we must not rely on the unsteady foundation of our own righteousness, but upon the foundation of the Rock, Christ.

The Gospel inspires us to hope in the Lord, because of the rich mercy and superabundant redemption in Him. This hope of the Gospel is an anchor of the soul, dependable, and faithful. The faith and delight of this hope is to remain firm and unyielding. Since the Gospel is the same which has been preached everywhere, we can depend upon the truth of it and should by no means depart from it.

ABBA Father, what or who in this world is against me or working for evil? I commit it to you and give thanks beforehand that you will turn it for good.

Father, help me to know the difference between waiting for you and simply waiting because I don't dare to move forward. Help me to seek your timing in all that I do.

Your Word says without faith it is impossible to please you. Thank you for my measure of faith to successfully walk my Christian journey. Amen.

Everlasting Love

Jeremiah 31:3 (MEV): *The Lord has appeared to him from afar, saying: Indeed, I have loved you with an everlasting love; therefore with lovingkindness I have drawn you.*

2 Thessalonians 2:16-17 (MEV): *Now may our Lord Jesus Christ Himself, and God our Father, who has loved us and has given us eternal consolation and good hope through grace, comfort your hearts and establish you in every good word and work.*

1 John 4:15-17: *If anyone acknowledges that Jesus is the Son of God, God lives in them and they in God. And so we know and rely on the love God has for us. God is love. Whoever lives in love lives in God, and God in them. This is how love is made complete among us so that we will have confidence on the day of judgment: In this world we are like Jesus.*

God has a heart to give and will give good things unto His children. The Father has loved us with an everlasting and unchangeable love and called us by His grace and adopted us into His family.

Christ has loved us with the same love which He shows by His continued intercession on our behalf. We are established in the love of God, in the covenant of grace, and in the arms of Christ, so they can never be removed.

ABBA Father, forgive me when I do not know how to love. I am so grateful that absolutely nothing can separate me from your everlasting love. Help me to show this same love to everyone around me. Help me to strive to be more about what love is than what it is not. Bless the people I love today. Amen.

Present and Future

Jeremiah 29:11 (MEV): *For I know the plans that I have for you, says the Lord, plans for peace and not for evil, to give you a future and a hope.*

2 Corinthians 4:17-18 (MEV): *Our light affliction, which lasts but for a moment, works for us a far more exceeding and eternal weight of glory, while we do not look at the things which are seen, but at the things which are not seen. For the things which are seen are temporal, but the things which are not seen are eternal.*

1 Thessalonians 1:2-3 (MEV): *We give thanks to God always for you all, mentioning you in our prayers, remembering without ceasing your work of faith, labor of love, and patient hope in our Lord Jesus Christ in the sight of God and our Father.*

Jesus Christ is the object of our faith, hope, and love. We can have enduring hope, not only because of what He has done in the past as our Savior but because of what He is doing in the present as our High Priest and what He will do in the future because of His promises and His character. Through the Apostle Paul's example, we see that it is our duty to be thankful for each other on a constant basis. It is difficult to be upset with someone while at the same time thanking God that he is our brother in Christ.

Dear Jesus, thank you for hearing my prayers for my present circumstances and future expectations. What gifts, resources, and abilities do I possess? I turn each one into a blessing to be given.

Father, grant me the wisdom to use my own good sense in the things I do and say. Help me to trust myself to make good decisions because I have put all my choices in your hands. I have the mind of Christ and hold the thoughts, feelings, and purposes of His heart. I have hope that you will work everything out for my good because of your love. Amen.

The Right Answer

John 5:39-40: *You study the Scriptures diligently because you think that in them you have eternal life. These are the very Scriptures that testify about me, yet you refuse to come to me to have life.*

2 Timothy 3:14-17 (MEV): *But continue in the things that you have learned and have been assured of, knowing those from whom you have learned them, and that since childhood you have known the Holy Scriptures, which are able to make you wise unto salvation through the faith that is in Christ Jesus. All Scripture is inspired by God and is profitable for teaching, for reproof, for correction, and for instruction in righteousness, that the man of God may be complete, thoroughly equipped for every good work.*

1 Peter 3:15 (MEV): *But sanctify the Lord God in your hearts. Always be ready to give an answer to every man who asks you for a reason for the hope that is in you, with gentleness and fear.*

Every Christian should be capable of defending the Gospel by being knowledgeable about the foundation of the Christian teachings. We should be always ready to share the Gospel and the importance of it. Therefore, it must become a daily and diligent search of the scriptures, meditate on them.

Give help and assistance to lead others into an understanding of the scriptures. The Lord God is blessed and honored when we share the truth of the Gospel and do not conceal it to please men.

ABBA Father, I am grateful that I can rely on your Word which is the only truth that will last forever. Father, your words are top priority to me. They are life. I let your Word dwell in me richly in all wisdom. The power of life and death is released through me by the words of my mouth. Therefore, I speak your words out of my mouth because they are alive in me. Amen.

God Is My Rock

Deuteronomy 32:3-4 (MEV): *For I will proclaim the name of the Lord: Ascribe greatness to our God! He is the Rock; His work is perfect; for all His ways are just. He is a God of faithfulness and without injustice; righteous and upright is He.*

2 Samuel 22:1-3 (MEV): *Now on the day the Lord delivered him from the hand of all of his enemies and from the hand of Saul, David spoke to the Lord the words of this song. He said: The Lord is my rock and my fortress and my deliverer; the God of my strength, in whom I will trust; my shield and the horn of my salvation, my fortress and my sanctuary; my Savior, You save me from violence.*

Psalm 62:5-6 (MEV): *My soul waits silently for God, for my hope is from Him. He only is my rock and my salvation; He is my refuge; I will not be moved.*

According to Psalm 62, King David's soul began to be uneasy and impatient. He encourages it to be still and quiet as he waits patiently on the Lord. The grace to have patience and hope is from the Lord and the thing hoped for is from Him. Therefore, we all can expect good things from the Lord. Our expectations in Him and His Word cannot fail and this is the reason why we should wait only on the Lord. Our faith gets fresh strength the more we consider God as our rock, salvation, and refuge.

ABBA Father, I am thankful that you alone are my rock, salvation, and refuge during my times of trouble. I have the expectation that you will bring me through victoriously for your glory.

Today, I practice seeing through the darkness of every problem or evil that confronts me to the good that lies beyond it. Father, you are the Holy One. You deserve all my worship and praise. You are without an equal. So high, so great, and so perfect are you.

I thank you for sending Jesus Christ, your Holy Son, to the cross that His holiness was imparted on me, that I might someday dwell with you and behold you in your majestic holiness. Help me to be holy. Let me dwell in your presence, my Holy One. Amen.

Deliverance Is Near

2 Samuel 22:2-3 (MEV): *He said: The Lord is my rock and my fortress and my deliverer; the God of my strength, in whom I will trust; my shield and the horn of my salvation, my fortress and my sanctuary; my Savior, You save me from violence.*

Psalm 39:7-8 (MEV): *Now, Lord, what do I wait for? My hope is in You. Deliver me from all my transgressions; do not make me the reproach of the foolish.*

Luke 4:18-19 (MEV): *The Spirit of the Lord is upon Me, because He has anointed Me to preach the Gospel to the poor; He has sent Me to heal the brokenhearted, to preach deliverance to the captives and recovery of sight to the blind, to set at liberty those who are oppressed; to preach the acceptable year of the Lord.*

Oftentimes, we look for or expect long life, but the days of men are so short. The world can see us completely useless without riches, but the riches of this world are temporary and fading away, but not the glories of Heaven.

The joy of the Lord is the focus of our hope and trust, the expectation of all good things, and this is the hope which brings contentment. Therefore, we must pray to the Lord for deliverance from all transgressions, knowing that if one of them was left to have control over us or the guilt that comes with them, we will be forever miserable. The Lord can and will deliver us out of all troubles caused by wicked men.

ABBA Father, hear my cry and see my tears. Today, I seek to find the riches of my faith and my identity as your child.

Father, thank you for giving me the choice every day to love you and serve you. Help me always to choose your ways. I fear not, for you have given me a spirit of power, of love, and of a sound mind. I put my trust in you to deliver and strengthen me. Amen.

The Glory

Psalm 24:7-8 (MEV): *Lift up your heads, O you gates; and be lifted up, you everlasting doors, that the King of glory may enter. Who is this King of glory? The Lord strong and mighty, the Lord mighty in battle.*

Colossians 1:27-28 (MEV): *To them God would make known what the glorious riches of this mystery among the nations is. It is Christ in you, the hope of glory, whom we preach, warning everyone and teaching everyone in all wisdom, so that we may present them perfect in Christ Jesus.*

2 Thessalonians 2:13-14 (MEV): *But we are bound to always give thanks to God for you, beloved brothers of the Lord, because God has from the beginning called you to salvation through sanctification by the Spirit and belief of the truth. To this He called you by our Gospel, to obtain the glory of our Lord Jesus Christ.*

The Gospel contains rich truths, a great treasure of them comparable to gold, silver, and precious stones. It contains rich promises, relating both to this life and that which is to come.

Christ is the riches of the Gospel; the rich blessings of it are all in His hands: righteousness, peace, love, grace, and mercy. Christ is also the glory of the Gospel because He is the author, preacher, and subject of it. Furthermore, the glory of God is expressed in Him, the glory of His wisdom, power, truth, and faithfulness. We shall have that glory with Christ, and everlasting communion with Him to all eternity, which is brought to light in the Gospel.

ABBA Father, I thank you for the rich truths of the Gospel. Please increase my knowledge of your will in all wisdom to boldly share the Gospel with the world. I love you, Father, and praise you for you are God and there is none else. Help me in this world that demands so much of my time and energy never to forget my need to worship you. Amen.

Don't Be Discouraged

Deuteronomy 31:6-8 (KJ21): *Be strong and of good courage, fear not, nor be afraid of them; for the Lord thy God, He it is who doth go with thee. He will not fail thee nor forsake thee. And Moses called unto Joshua and said unto him in the sight of all Israel, "Be strong and of good courage; for thou must go with this people unto the land which the Lord hath sworn unto their fathers to give them, and thou shalt cause them to inherit it. And the Lord, He it is who doth go before thee. He will be with thee, He will not fail thee, neither forsake thee. Fear not, neither be dismayed."*

Joshua 1:9 (KJ21): *Have not I commanded thee? Be strong and of a good courage; be not afraid, neither be thou dismayed, for the Lord thy God is with thee whithersoever thou goest.*

Psalm 31:24 (KJ21): *Be of good courage, and He shall strengthen your heart, all ye that hope in the Lord.*

As the result of all his own experience of the goodness of God and his conflicts with danger, the psalmist encourages us that God will never leave or forsake us. God will equip you to meet trials and keep you from becoming weak and discouraged.

When we put all of our trust and expectations in God, we cannot be disappointed. It is a characteristic of true devotion that all hope centers on God. God alone can give success that will be good for our families and bless the world. Hope in God encourages, supports, and makes our lives joyful and prosperous.

ABBA Father, I will only put my trust in you. Father, you are my deliverer; lead and guide me through my trials. I tread upon serpents, scorpions, and over all the power of the enemy. I take my shield of faith and quench his fiery darts.

Father, grant me a heart of wisdom so that all the works of my hands will reflect a willing and loving heart. Greater is He that is in me than he that is in the world. Thank you for loving and strengthening me. Amen.

The Good News

Isaiah 61:1-3 (ESV): *The Spirit of the Lord God is upon me, because the Lord has anointed me to bring good news to the poor; he has sent me to bind up the brokenhearted, to proclaim liberty to the captives, and the opening of the prison to those who are bound; to proclaim the year of the Lord's favor, and the day of vengeance of our God; to comfort all who mourn; to grant to those who mourn in Zion—to give them a beautiful headdress instead of ashes, the oil of gladness instead of mourning, the garment of praise instead of a faint spirit; that they may be called oaks of righteousness, the planting of the Lord, that he may be glorified.*

Colossians 1:5-6 (ERV): *Your faith and love continue because you know what is waiting for you in heaven—the hope you have had since you first heard the true message, the Good News that was told to you. Throughout the world, this Good News is bringing blessings and is spreading. And that's what has been happening among you since the first time you heard it and understood the truth about God's grace.*

Luke 2:9-11 (ERV): *An angel of the Lord appeared to them, and the glory of the Lord was shining around them. The shepherds were very afraid. The angel said to them, "Don't be afraid. I have some very good news for you—news that will make everyone happy. Today your Savior was born in David's town. He is the Messiah, the Lord.*

All Christians should display faithfulness through every relationship. Faith, hope, and love are the three principal graces in the Christian life. The more we fix our hopes on our reward in Heaven, the freer we can be in doing good with our earthly treasure. The Gospel is the Word of truth, and all who hear the Gospel should bring forth the fruit of the Gospel by obeying it and live according to it.

ABBA Father, I repent of anything not in your will. I dwell in the comfort of your presence where my miracles await.

Father, forgive the past moments where I was not wise or aware of you and bless me today, right where I am, and keep me close to you. I commit to being fruitful in every good work and let my faithfulness be pleasing to you. Amen.

Safety From Harm

Psalm 121:5-8: *The Lord watches over you—the Lord is your shade at your right hand; the sun will not harm you by day, nor the moon by night. The Lord will keep you from all harm—he will watch over your life; the Lord will watch over your coming and going both now and forevermore.*

Job 5:15-16 (ERV): *God saves the poor from the hurtful words of the wicked. He saves them from those who are powerful. So, the poor have hope; God shuts the mouths of those who would cause them harm.*

2 Thessalonians 3:2-3: *And pray that we may be delivered from wicked and evil people, for not everyone has faith. But the Lord is faithful, and he will strengthen you and protect you from the evil one.*

The Lord saves those from the dishonest and scheming, from their enemies who set traps, and lie in wait to draw them in. God takes notice and saves them from their enemies who speak evil which destroys their credit and reputation, then threatens them with ruin. Therefore, through the revelation of the grace and mercy of God, they have a hope of safety in Christ Jesus and they will receive eternal life through Him, a promise from God.

ABBA Father, what is the direction of the calling of my life? Today, I dwell only on that which leads to that destination and on nothing that doesn't. I am delivered from this present evil world. I am seated with Christ Jesus in Heavenly places. I reside in the Kingdom of God.

The law of the spirit of life in Christ Jesus has made me free from the law of sin and death. Thank you that I have a shelter of safety with you. I know and trust that you will deliver me from all the traps of the evil one. Amen.

The Inheritance

Ephesians 1:18: *I pray that the eyes of your heart may be enlightened in order that you may know the hope to which he has called you, the riches of his glorious inheritance in his holy people, ...*

Colossians 1:9-12: *For this reason, since the day we heard about you, we have not stopped praying for you. We continually ask God to fill you with the knowledge of his will through all the wisdom and understanding that the Spirit gives, so that you may live a life worthy of the Lord and please him in every way: bearing fruit in every good work, growing in the knowledge of God, being strengthened with all power according to his glorious might so that you may have great endurance and patience, and giving joyful thanks to the Father, who has qualified you to share in the inheritance of his holy people in the kingdom of light.*

1 Peter 1:3-5: *Praise be to the God and Father of our Lord Jesus Christ! In his great mercy he has given us new birth into a living hope through the resurrection of Jesus Christ from the dead, and into an inheritance that can never perish, spoil, or fade. This inheritance is kept in heaven for you, who through faith are shielded by God's power until the coming of the salvation that is ready to be revealed in the last time.*

In one of his letters, the apostle prays for his readers to receive a greater understanding of their calling from God. God calls with a holy calling, which is an encouragement for the hope of eternal life. The apostle prays that these saints, who were called by the grace of God, might know more of Christ, the foundation of their hope, and what they are hoping for. The Heavenly inheritance is an eternal gift: it is not only identified by beautiful mansions but by a kingdom with riches and glory, which cannot be fully known in this life.

ABBA Father, help me to follow your Word which says for me *not to lay up for myself treasures on earth, where moth and rust corrupt and where thieves break in and steal. I should lay up for myself treasures in Heaven, for where my treasure is, there will be my heart.*

The Blood of the Lamb breaks every chain and bondage. I walk today in the power of the Lamb and break free. I hear the voice of the Good Shepherd. I hear my ABBA Father's voice and the voice of a stranger I will not follow. I throw my cares upon God. I commit and trust them wholly to Him. He will cause my thoughts to become agreeable to His will and so shall my plans be established and succeed. Amen.

All My Help

Psalm 146:5-6: *Blessed are those whose help is the God of Jacob whose hope is in the Lord their God. He is the Maker of heaven and earth, the sea, and everything in them—he remains faithful forever.*

Isaiah 41:10-13: *So do not fear, for I am with you; do not be dismayed, for I am your God. I will strengthen you and help you; I will uphold you with my righteous right hand. All who rage against you will surely be ashamed and disgraced; those who oppose you will be as nothing and perish. Though you search for your enemies, you will not find them. Those who wage war against you will be as nothing at all. For I am the Lord your God who takes hold of your right hand and says to you, Do not fear; I will help you.*

Hebrews 13:5-7: *Keep your lives free from the love of money and be content with what you have, because God has said, "Never will I leave you; never will I forsake you." So we say with confidence, "The Lord is my helper; I will not be afraid. What can mere mortals do to me?" Remember your leaders, who spoke the word of God to you. Consider the outcome of their way of life and imitate their faith.*

Now happy is everyone that has God for their help. God helps all His people from all their infirmities, temptations, and afflictions. He helps them to all the blessings of grace and helps them to everlasting glory and happiness.

Now happy is everyone whose help and hope alone is in Christ Jesus, which is the reason for faith and hope in Him. All things are made by Him, which are in the whole span of creation. He must be the mighty God, the truth of every promise in His Holy Word, and He will see them accomplished.

ABBA Father, today I believe and take courage to live confidently in the truth that your goodwill, in the end, prevails over all evil in the world and in my life.

Father, I want to share your love with others. Thank you for protecting me and equipping me for this task. I praise you for being my faithful help whenever I am in need. I trust you because your Word says that nothing can or will separate me from your love. Amen.

Feed Your Soul

Deuteronomy 4:29-31 (MEV): *But if from there you will seek the Lord your God, you will find Him, if you seek Him with all your heart and with all your soul. When you are in distress and all these things come upon you, even in the latter days, if you turn to the Lord your God and shall be obedient to His voice (for the Lord your God is a merciful God), He will not abandon you or destroy you or forget the covenant of your fathers which He swore to them.*

Psalm 42:5 (MEV): *Why are you cast down, O my soul? And why are you disquieted in me? Hope in God, for I will yet thank Him for the help of His presence.*

3 John 1:2-3 (MEV): *Beloved, I pray that all may go well with you and that you may be in good health, even as your soul is well. For I greatly rejoiced when brothers came and testified of the truth that is in you, just as you walk in the truth.*

Have you ever asked the following questions:

- Will these present troubles last forever?
- Why should I believe God will bring to pass what He has promised?

Oftentimes, when we are depressed and fearful it springs from unbelief. Put your hope and trust in God.

God is unchangeable and, therefore, His grace is the ground for unshaken hope. Hope has a powerful influence on the Christian during afflictions. Hope fills the afflicted soul with such inward joy and comfort that it can laugh while tears are in the eyes; sigh and sing all in a breath.

Let us spend less time in questioning and more time in strengthening our souls. If we do so, we will receive mercy from God and He deserves our praise.

ABBA Father, it is such a comfort to know that your eyes watch over me and that your ears hear my cries for help. Thank you for hearing my cries and for rescuing me when I am crushed in spirit.

Today, I get rid of the distractions and return to you, ABBA Father. I praise you, ABBA Father, for the hope and courage your promises give me when I am face-to-face with the most difficult of circumstances. Please forgive me when I walk ahead of you. Help me to always stay close by your side. Father, I know you love me and I say let your will be done in my life as it is in Heaven. Amen.

More Than A Conqueror

Isaiah 40:29-31: *He gives strength to the weary and increases the power of the weak. Even youths grow tired and weary, and young men stumble and fall; but those who hope in the Lord will renew their strength. They will soar on wings like eagles; they will run and not grow weary they will walk and not be faint.*

Ephesians 6:10-12: *Finally, be strong in the Lord and in his mighty power. Put on the full armor of God, so that you can take your stand against the devil's schemes. For our struggle is not against flesh and blood, but against the rulers, against the authorities, against the powers of this dark world and against the spiritual forces of evil in the heavenly realms.*

Philippians 4:13: *I can do all this through him who gives me strength.*

Oftentimes, we are ready to faint under afflictions because immediate deliverance has not come. Our prayers are not answered at once or promises are not fulfilled as expected. According to scripture, God gives fresh supplies of spiritual strength. He strengthens our faith, enlarges our views to behold His goodness, and confirms His blessings and promises of grace.

Therefore, let us wait and rely upon the Lord for strength to bear our burdens. We will have deliverance from them in due time. We will grow stronger and stronger in faith, patience, and courage, whereby we can be more than conquerors over all enemies and troubles.

ABBA Father, today I journey away from the familiar to the new as I seek more of you, your will, and your presence. Father, I thank you for calling me to be a fellow workman and a laborer with you. I commit to pray and not give up.

Jesus, you are the Son of God and I will never stop trusting you. You are my High Priest and you understand my weaknesses. So I come boldly to the throne of my gracious ABBA Father. There I receive mercy, find grace, and help when I need it. I am grateful and it is a comfort to know that you will renew my strength to go through my storms and become more than a conqueror. Amen.

Pursue The Prince Of Peace

Psalm 29:11 (MEV): *The Lord will give strength to His people; the Lord will bless His people with peace.*

Isaiah 26:3 (MEV): *You will keep him in perfect peace, whose mind is stayed on You, because he trusts in You.*

John 14:27 (MEV): *Peace I leave with you. My peace I give to you. Not as the world gives do I give to you. Let not your heart be troubled, neither let it be afraid.*

One of the purposes of the Gospel is to raise up hope and faith in the servants of God as well as keep their minds and hearts from the world. The ultimate goal is to raise them to Heaven and the things above.

How excellent then is the Gospel, which consists of divine promises? Faith comes by hearing and hearing by the Word of God. Whosoever is appointed and called must preach the Word. Grace is the free favor of God, acceptance with Him, and the fountain of all blessings. Mercy is the fruit of the favor and peace is the effect and fruit of mercy. Therefore, accept peace with God through Christ who is our peace.

ABBA Father, today I make it my aim to receive the peace of Jesus, the fullness of rest, completion, well-being, and wholeness. I have on the breastplate of righteousness, which is faith and love. My feet are shod with the preparation of the Gospel of peace. In Christ Jesus I have peace. I am a minister of reconciliation, proclaiming the Good News of the Gospel. I thank you that, through faith, I have grace, mercy, and peace. Amen.

Praises

Psalm 47:6-7 (MEV): *Sing praises to God, sing praises; sing praises to our King, sing praises. For God is the King of all the earth; sing praises with understanding.*

Psalm 100:4 (MEV): *Enter into His gates with thanksgiving, and into His courts with praise; be thankful to Him and bless His name.*

Hebrews 13:15-16 (MEV): *Through Him, then, let us continually offer to God the sacrifice of praise, which is the fruit of our lips, giving thanks to His name. But do not forget to do good and to share. For with such sacrifices God is well pleased.*

The Lord takes pleasure in everyone that serves and worships Him, privately and publicly, with reverence and love. His heart is full of love, and compassion toward them.

The Lord displays goodness and communicates the mysteries of His Word, love, and grace. In those that hope in the absolute mercy of God, they will obtain, in their hearts, blessings of grace and salvation. The Lord desires to have an eternal relationship with anyone who is seeking Him.

DEVOTIONAL

ABBA Father, I am grateful for your unfailing love towards me. I sing to you because you deserve all my praises. Holy, Holy, Holy, art you, Jehovah God. I join with all of creation to praise and worship your name.

Forgive me if I have grieved you; make my heart clean that I may walk with you and receive the blessing of your presence. I glorify your name and pray that you will give me a greater understanding of your wonderful Word. Amen.

The Comforter

Psalm 119:81-82: *My soul faints with longing for your salvation, but I have put my hope in your word. My eyes fail, looking for your promise; I say, "When will you comfort me?"*

John 14:25-26 (YLT): *These things I have spoken to you, remaining with you, and the Comforter, the Holy Spirit, whom the Father will send in my name, he will teach you all things, and remind you of all things that I said to you.*

2 Corinthians 1:3-4: *Praise be to the God and Father of our Lord Jesus Christ, the Father of compassion and the God of all comfort, who comforts us in all our troubles, so that we can comfort those in any trouble with the comfort we ourselves receive from God.*

King David, in Psalm 119, expected from the Lord salvation and deliverance from his enemies. His spirit began to sink and faint as he waited for the promise of joy and comfort. King David's eyes grew weary and he was ready to give up all expectations of comfort. Oftentimes, we are inclined to think God is taking too long and inquire how much longer will we have to wait as King David did. But God is faithful to what He has promised and is able to perform. His Word lays a solid foundation for faith and hope, however, when we are discouraged and need comforting, we must seek God. He alone can comfort and has His set times to do it.

ABBA Father, you and your Word are faithful. Today I leave the "realm of doubt" and go beyond to the bare truth of Jesus' presence. I'll be still and know that He is my Comforter.

Father, thank you for loving me and rejoicing over me. The spirit of rejoicing and laughter is my heritage. Where your Spirit is there is liberty. I will walk in that liberty. I seek your comfort and strength as I am surrounded by trouble. Because of your loving-kindness, I know you are my God of hope. Amen.

The Eyes Of The Lord

Psalm 33:18 (MEV): *The eyes of the Lord is on those who fear Him, on those who hope in His lovingkindness.*

Proverbs 15:3 (MEV): *The eyes of the Lord are in every place, keeping watch on the evil and the good.*

1 Peter 3:12 (MEV): *For the eyes of the Lord are on the righteous, and His ears are open to their prayers; but the face of the Lord is against those who do evil.*

We must be careful not to offend God but to serve and worship Him. Daily, His eyes with love and grace are to protect us from danger and to supply us with the essentials of life.

The Lord looks, with delight and pleasure, by His mercy through Christ. His mission to this world gave us deliverance, salvation, and eternal life. The eyes of the Lord are on those who are in need and encouraged to hope in the heart of God.

ABBA Father, today, I take your Word and plant it in the soil of my heart. I let your Word bear fruit in my life. Jesus, you are the Bridegroom that Father promises. Thank you for assuring me that even now you are preparing a place for me in Heaven. I am grateful that you are seated high above the earth to see everything. This gives me hope to patiently wait for your help. I love you, Father, and my heart can rejoice for my trust is in you. Amen.

Dreams Do Come True!

Genesis 28:12-13 (MEV): *He dreamed and saw a ladder set up on the earth with the top of it reaching to heaven. The angels of God were ascending and descending on it. The Lord stood above it and said, I am the Lord God of Abraham your father and the God of Isaac. The land on which you lie, to you will I give it and to your descendants.*

1 Kings 3:5, 9, 12 (MEV): *While he was in Gibeon, the Lord appeared to Solomon in a dream at night, and He said, "Ask what you want from Me." "Give Your servant therefore an understanding heart to judge Your people, that I may discern between good and bad, for who is able to judge among so great a people?" "I now do according to your words. I have given you a wise and an understanding heart, so that there has never been anyone like you in the past, and there shall never arise another like you."*

Proverbs 13:12 (TPT): *When hope's dream seems to drag on and on, the delay can be depressing. But when at last your dream comes true, life's sweetness will satisfy your soul.*

The mind becomes uneasy when what is hoped for does not come as soon as expected. The heart sinks and fails if what we hoped for is delayed by any length of time.

Oftentimes, we are discouraged and ready to give up all hope of enjoying the desired dream. However, when the long-desired comes to fruition, there is unspeakable pleasure and delight. Christ's work of redemption and salvation came and brought blessings with Him.

Dear Jesus, I live this day after the pattern of always receiving and giving. I live to be a blessing in the flowing of your love. My heart is so heavy, sometimes, that I cannot bear the waiting for the manifestation of my dreams. I ask for your strength and your peace as I wait for your answers.

Thank you, Jesus, for your many blessings which are sweet to my soul. I know when I hear and obey your commandments, there is an eternal reward in Heaven. Amen.

Heavenly Home

Psalm 37:8-9: *Refrain from anger and turn from wrath; do not fret—it leads only to evil. For those who are evil will be destroyed, but those who hope in the Lord will inherit the land.*

John 3:16-17: *For God so loved the world that he gave his one and only Son, that whoever believes in him shall not perish but have eternal life. For God did not send his Son into the world to condemn the world, but to save the world through him.*

1 John 5:13-14: *I write these things to you who believe in the name of the Son of God so that you may know that you have eternal life. This is the confidence we have in approaching God: that if we ask anything according to his will, he hears us.*

Psalm 37 is advising the readers to cease anger either at wicked men who are prosperous or at God. Envying or imitating the wicked in hope of being prosperous as they are may lead to evil. Though they flourish for a while, they shall be cut down like the grass or flower of the field. They shall be cut off as branches from a blooming tree; they shall be cut off from the earth.

When we obey the Word of the Lord, worship, and trust in His grace and mercy, we will see the manifestations of His promises. The promises are that, through Christ, we are joint-heirs with Him and enjoy the blessings of answered prayers, supplies of grace, and live in the expectation of the Heavenly glory. Those that wait upon the Lord and trust in Him, will dwell in the Heavenly country, the inheritance.

ABBA Father, thank you for directing my steps. I might fall, but I trust that your mighty hand will pick me up. I'm grateful for the promise that if I wait on you and keep your ways, I will receive my inheritance of eternal life with you. I dwell on the blessings of the place being prepared for me.

Father, I will not draw back or shrink in fear for then you would have no delight or pleasure in me. I was bought for a price, purchased with a preciousness, and made your very own. I honor and bring glory to you. Amen.

The Divine High Priest

Genesis 14:18 (MEV): *Then Melchizedek king of Salem brought out bread and wine. He was the priest of God Most High.*

Psalm 110:1, 4 (AMPC): *The Lord (God) says to my Lord (the Messiah), Sit at My right hand, until I make Your adversaries Your footstool. The Lord has sworn and will not revoke or change it: You are a priest forever, after the manner and order of Melchizedek.*

Hebrews 8:1-2 (MEV): *Now this is the main point of the things that we are saying: We have such a High Priest, who is seated at the right hand of the throne of the Majesty in the heavens, a minister in the sanctuary and the true tabernacle, which the Lord, not man, set up.*

The Levitical priesthood could not bring men into fellowship with God. Therefore, Jesus in His becoming High Priest, brought a better hope and better promises by which we come close to God. Even the Jew, who would have considered a change of the priestly line impossible, expected perfection only when Messiah appeared. In the law, the priests were those who came near unto God, and now that opportunity belongs to all God's people.

ABBA Father, Jesus' death was the death of my old life. I give that which is old a eulogy and a burial. I'm finished with it and I am free.

Father, thank you for the New Covenant which has given Jesus as our High Priest forever. Thank you, Jesus, as High Priest sitting on the right hand of our Father, for making daily intercessions on our behalf. Jesus, you truly are the Lion of Judah, the Mightiest of all, King of kings and Lord of lords. I bow and worship at your throne. Amen.

Walk In Truth

Psalm 25:5: *Guide me in your truth and teach me, for you are God my Savior, and my hope is in you all day long.*

1 Corinthians 13:6-7: *Love does not delight in evil but rejoices with the truth. It always protects, always trusts, always hopes, always perseveres.*

1 John 3:18-20: *Dear children, let us not love with words or speech but with actions and in truth. This is how we know that we belong to the truth and how we set our hearts at rest in his presence: If our hearts condemn us, we know that God is greater than our hearts, and he knows everything.*

God is troubled at the evilness of the world and He does not rejoice at any unjust action or injury. He rejoices in the truth of the Gospel and its success. God rejoices greatly when He sees His children walking in truth and standing against wickedness.

Christians are to believe and have hope in all things that God says in His Word. We must trust in all His truths and the accomplishment of all His promises including hope for things that are not seen and are difficult but possible according to God's Word. We must place our hope in Heaven and eternal happiness. We must hope for the best of all men, even of wicked men, and that they may find God's truth.

ABBA Father, I say goodbye to my sins, guilt, and past. I let it go and cut it off forever. Father, I am truly in awe of you and the wonders of the world that you've created.

Thank you for making me just as I am. Your love has been shed abroad in my heart by the Holy Spirit and His love abides in me richly. I keep myself in the Kingdom of Light, in love, in the Word, and the wicked one touches me not. I'm grateful that your love never fails. Today, I rejoice while walking in your truth that through love I will be victorious. Amen.

The Kingdom Of Heaven

Matthew 4:23 (TPT): *Jesus ministered from place to place throughout all the province of Galilee. He taught in the synagogues, preaching the hope of the kingdom realm, and healing every kind of sickness and disease among the people.*

Mark 1:14-15 (MEV): *After John was put in prison, Jesus came to Galilee preaching the Gospel of the kingdom of God, saying, "The time is fulfilled, and the kingdom of God is at hand. Repent and believe the Gospel."*

Acts 28:23 (TPT): *So they set a time to meet with Paul. On that day, an even greater crowd gathered where he was staying. From morning until evening Paul taught them, opening up the truths of God's kingdom realm. With convincing arguments from both the Law and the Prophets, he tried to persuade them about Jesus.*

The Apostle Matthew reminds us that Jesus not only prayed and read the Scriptures in the synagogues, but He also preached. Jesus went throughout Galilee declaring messages of His grace and the Kingdom of Heaven. He encouraged those assembled to repent and abandon their former teachings and to receive the things concerning the Kingdom of Heaven: *except a man be born again, he cannot see it and he cannot enter it.*

Jesus also healed every sickness and every disease among the people. Let us follow the example of Jesus: pray, read the Scriptures, and preached about the Kingdom of Heaven.

Dear Jesus, today instead of trying to reach you, I let you reach me, just where I am, just as I am. Thank you for your presence. You are always there when I need you. Without your presence, life would not be worth living. Your presence brings joy and hope to my life.

Thank you for your ministry on this earth. Jesus, you declared that greater works your followers would do. Please help me to be more like you to teach and preach about the Kingdom of Heaven. Amen.

Thankful In Prayer

Philippians 4:6-7: *Do not be anxious about anything, but in every situation, by prayer and petition, with thanksgiving, present your requests to God. And the peace of God, which transcends all understanding, will guard your hearts and your minds in Christ Jesus.*

Colossians 4:2-4: *Devote yourselves to prayer, being watchful and thankful. And pray for us, too, that God may open a door for our message, so that we may proclaim the mystery of Christ, for which I am in chains. Pray that I may proclaim it clearly, as I should.*

1 Thessalonians 5:16-18: *Rejoice always, pray continually, give thanks in all circumstances; for this is God's will for you in Christ Jesus.*

Apostle Paul professes hope in prayer, concerning himself, his companions, and his ministry. He expresses the intense desires of his heart after God and his affection for Him. Apostle Paul is waiting for the Lord's deliverance out of the depths of distress. God has His set time for the fulfillment of the promises He had made to him. Apostle Paul can confidently expect all his prayers to be answered since God is gracious, merciful, wise, powerful, faithful, and unchangeable.

ABBA Father, I come today taking the shield of faith, wherewith I'm able to quench all the fiery darts of the wicked; the helmet of salvation (holding the thoughts, feelings, and purposes of Your heart); and the Sword of the Spirit which is Your Word. In the face of all trials, tests, and temptations, I cut to pieces the snare of the enemy by speaking your Word.

Thank you for hearing my voice when I cry out. My hope is your word that you will never leave or forsake me in my times of trouble. Amen.

The High Calling

2 Corinthians 6:18 (MEV): *"I will be a Father to you, and you shall be My sons and daughters, says the Lord Almighty."*

Matthew 5:9 (MEV): *Blessed are the peacemakers, for they shall be called the sons of God.*

1 John 3:1-3 (MEV): *Consider how much love the Father has given to us, that we should be called children of God. Therefore, the world does not know us, because it did not know Him. Beloved, now are we children of God, and it has not yet been revealed what we shall be. But we know that when He appears, we shall be like Him, for we shall see Him as He is. Everyone who has this hope in Him purifies himself, just as He is pure.*

Little does the world know of the happiness of real followers of Christ. The real followers of Christ have an expectation of seeing Him. This expectation is built on a solid foundation of being a child of God.

As a child of God, we must, with a believing heart, earnestly pray and exercise faith in the truths and promises of the Gospel. The person who is inspired by this well-grounded hope will keep the pure and holy character of Christ before his or her eyes.

Hope is that we will receive the prize of the high calling of God in Christ Jesus. It is God's will and pleasure that believers should be conformed to the image of His Son in order to have the high honor and great happiness of dwelling with Him forever.

ABBA Father, thank you for the love that is expressed by calling me your child. I open my heart to receive overflowing rivers of your compassion and love. Help me to live today in constant awareness of my position as a joint heir with Jesus Christ.

Father, I commit today to follow Jesus and to love others, not just in words but in my actions and in truth. Amen.

A Living Hope

Jeremiah 17:7 (MEV): *Blessed is the man who trusts in the Lord, and whose hope is the Lord.*

Titus 3:4-7 (CEV): *God our Savior showed us how good and kind he is. He saved us because of his mercy, and not because of any good things that we have done. God washed us by the power of the Holy Spirit. He gave us new birth and a fresh beginning. God sent Jesus Christ our Savior to give us his Spirit. Jesus treated us much better than we deserve. He made us acceptable to God and gave us the hope of eternal life.*

1 Peter 1:3 (MEV): *Blessed be the God and Father of our Lord Jesus Christ, who according to His abundant mercy has given us a new birth into a living hope through the resurrection of Jesus Christ from the dead.*

God, and His wonderful works, are a blessing to His children. We should give Him glory and express thanksgiving in our hearts and lives. God's great love and free favor, His rich grace, and abundant mercy are the moving cause of faith and hope. The grace of hope in a living Christ makes the heart of a believer cheerful and energetic and will never be lost but embraced forever. Therefore, Christ's resurrection is what lays a solid foundation of hope for eternal glory and happiness.

ABBA Father, I live today as if it was day one of my life; as if everything that should have never been, never was, and all is new. For in redemption, it is so.

I am a world overcomer because I am born of you. I represent you and Jesus well. I am a useful member of the Body of Christ. I am your workmanship recreated in Christ Jesus. I am grateful that your Word endures forever.

Thank you for your abundant mercy which gives me a living hope through Jesus Christ of eternal life with you. Amen.

Hope In The Future

Proverbs 24:14: *Know also that wisdom is like honey for you: If you find it, there is a future hope for you, and your hope will not be cut off.*

Jeremiah 29:11 (MEV): *For I know the plans that I have for you, says the Lord, plans for peace and not for evil, to give you a future and a hope.*

Romans 8:23-25 (MEV): *Not only that, but we also, who have the first fruits of the Spirit, groan within ourselves while eagerly waiting for adoption, the redemption of our bodies. For we are saved through hope, but hope that is seen is not hope, for why does a man still hope for what he sees? But if we hope for what we do not see, we wait for it with patience.*

The Christian who has received the gift of the Spirit is already an adopted child of God. But this adoption still must be perfected, which will not be until the Coming of Christ. Then the children of God will be transformed and cleared from all the imperfections of their earthly body and life.

Hope in the future is the basic nature of a Christian's life. However, we must have the faith to see the future, hope for it, and patiently endure the road to it.

ABBA Father, thank you that I am a joint heir with Christ. I apply today this most radical power to turn darkness into light, defeat into victory, and death into life. I start turning things upside down.

Father, I praise you with all my heart, mind, and soul as I celebrate your amazing gift of eternal life. I trust in the fact that this present time on earth is not worthy to be compared with the glory which will be revealed in Heaven. Amen.

The Priceless Gift

Titus 2:11-14 (MEV): *For the grace of God that brings salvation has appeared to all men, teaching us that, denying ungodliness and worldly desires, we should live soberly, righteously, and in godliness in this present world, as we await the blessed hope and the appearing of the glory of our great God and Savior Jesus Christ, who gave Himself for us, that He might redeem us from all lawlessness and purify for Himself a special people, zealous of good works.*

1 Corinthians 1:30 (MEV): *But because of Him you are in Christ Jesus, whom God made unto us wisdom, righteousness, sanctification, and redemption.*

Hebrews 9:15 (MEV): *For this reason He is the Mediator of a new covenant, since a death has occurred for the redemption of the sins that were committed under the first covenant, so that those who are called might receive the promise of eternal inheritance.*

The Bible teaches that ungodliness, atheism, and all false religion are commonly found in the hearts of men. However, there is a blessed hope in the glorious appearance of our Savior Jesus Christ.

Christ was not only sent and given by the Father but freely gave up Himself to die for the world. He redeemed us from all iniquity, purchased salvation for us, and delivered us from the guilt and power of sin. Christ purified unto Himself a peculiar people. We should be zealous to do and pursue all good works that are acceptable to God and profitable to ourselves and others.

ABBA Father, thank you for your grace that brought salvation through our Savior Jesus Christ. I start this day by seeking first my actions and steps from you. My heartfelt and continued prayers through Christ's offering for my sins is that I have tremendous power available to accomplish your works. When I accomplish your works, it brings great glory to You. I live in you and your words continue to live in my heart.

Jesus, thank you for your priceless gift of redemption and the blessed hope of your soon return. Amen.

The Unforgettable God

Deuteronomy 8:19-20 (MEV): *If you ever forget the Lord your God and go after other gods and serve them and worship them, then I testify against you today that you will surely perish. Just like the nations which the Lord will destroy before you, so shall you perish because you would not be obedient to the voice of the Lord your God.*

Job 8:13-14 (MEV): *So are the paths of all who forget God; and the hypocrite's hope will perish, whose confidence will be cut off, and whose trust will be a spider's web.*

Isaiah 49:15-16 (MEV): *Can a woman forget her nursing child and have no compassion on the son of her womb? Even these may forget, yet I will not forget. See, I have inscribed you on the palms of My hands; your walls are continually before Me.*

Who forgets that there is a God and tries to live without Him in the world? Who forgets the glorious displays of God's creation? Who forgets the benefits and blessings of His goodness and is not thankful for them?

In the Book of Job, the hope and confidence of a person is compared to a spider's web: very thin and cannot bear any weight. The works of such persons are dependent on themselves and done without the grace of God. Though they may think themselves safe enclosed in their own works as in a house, they will find themselves terribly misguided. There is no shelter, safety, and security in such works. There is only shelter, safety, and security in Christ and His righteousness.

ABBA Father, even modern history bears witness that you are the God of the impossible. Seeing the reality, today I believe you for the impossible.

Father, I know you have blessed me. Help me to step out of the way and be willing to share my gifts and talents with others according to your will and purpose.

Today, I declare that I will not lean to my own understanding. I will not forget but acknowledge you in all my ways. Amen.

The Good Reward

Matthew 6:6 (ERV): *But when you pray, you should go into your room and close the door. Then pray to your Father. He is there in that private place. He can see what is done in private, and he will reward you.*

Colossians 3:23-24 (ERV): *In all the work you are given, do the best you can. Work as though you are working for the Lord, not any earthly master. Remember that you will receive your reward from the Lord, who will give you what he promised his people. Yes, you are serving Christ. He is your real Master.*

Hebrews 11:6 (ERV): *Without faith no one can please God. Whoever comes to God must believe that he is real and that he rewards those who sincerely try to find him.*

The righteous should never be envious of evil men's prosperity and worldly happiness. Those who choose to do evil will receive no reward of good things such as is for the righteous in a way of grace at the end of their lives.

The wicked have no hope of future things, no good hope of everlasting happiness. They have their good things now and their evil things hereafter. The wicked prosperity, riches, honor, and happiness in this life are a small comparison to those who choose to do good and receive the good reward of eternal life in Heaven.

ABBA Father, I ask you for wisdom to follow and obey your Word. I seek out that which will challenge me, stretch me, grow me, and strengthen me in you.

Father, wash away the weary thoughts that hold me back and fill me with your Spirit so that I might adopt a positive attitude and discover your miracles. Father, I choose to do good on this earth that I may receive your good and eternal reward in Heaven. Amen.

Equip For Battle

1 Thessalonians 5:8 (ERV): *But we belong to the day, so we should control ourselves. We should wear faith and love to protect us. And the hope of salvation should be our helmet.*

2 Timothy 4:7-8 (ERV): *I have fought the good fight. I have finished the race. I have served the Lord faithfully. Now, a prize is waiting for me—the crown that will show I am right with God. The Lord, the judge who judges rightly, will give it to me on that Day. Yes, he will give it to me and to everyone else who is eagerly looking forward to his coming.*

1 John 5:3-5 (ERV): *Loving God means obeying his commands. And God's commands are not too hard for us, because everyone who is a child of God has the power to win against the world. It is our faith that has won the victory against the world. So who wins against the world? Only those who believe that Jesus is the Son of God.*

These two graces go together: faith works by love and love always accompanies faith. Faith is an important part of the Christian soldier's breastplate. This breastplate surrounds the soul, protects it from the devil's temptations, and guards the heart against the wicked. For faith in the promises of God overcomes all the doubts that object to the fulfillment of them.

Love is the other part of the breastplate: love to God and Christ is a means of keeping the believer sound in the faith. A soul that loves God and Christ cannot give in to anything that devalues the grace of God, the glory of Christ, or the work of the Spirit.

The helmet is that part of the armor which covers the head on the day of battle and preserves it from being defeated by sin and the devil. A Christian clothed and armed with these graces of faith, hope, and love, should be so far from indulging in sin, always sober and watchful, and be ready and waiting for the Lord's coming.

DEVOTIONAL

ABBA Father, I give you praise for my Holy armor. I pray that my spirit, soul, and body be preserved blameless until the coming of Jesus Christ. Nothing can stop the one who walks fully in your will. I am that person and I break every chain and obstacle to the contrary.

Father, thank you for choosing me, picking me as your own in Christ Jesus before the foundation of the worlds, that I should be holy and blameless in your sight. Amen.

The Father's Gift

John 3:16-17 (AMPC): *For God so greatly loved and dearly prized the world that He [even] gave up His only begotten (unique) Son, so that whoever believes in (trusts in, clings to, relies on) Him shall not perish (come to destruction, be lost) but have eternal (everlasting) life. For God did not send the Son into the world in order to judge (to reject, to condemn, to pass sentence on) the world, but that the world might find salvation and be made safe and sound through Him.*

Titus 3:6-8 (CSB): *He poured out his Spirit on us abundantly through Jesus Christ our Savior so that, having been justified by his grace, we may become heirs with the hope of eternal life. This saying is trustworthy. I want you to insist on these things, so that those who have believed God might be careful to devote themselves to good works. These are good and profitable for everyone.*

1 John 5:10-13 (CSB): *The one who believes in the Son of God has this testimony within himself. The one who does not believe God has made him a liar, because he has not believed in the testimony God has given about his Son. And this is the testimony: God has given us eternal life, and this life is in his Son. The one who has the Son has life. The one who does not have the Son of God does not have life. I have written these things to you who believe in the name of the Son of God so that you may know that you have eternal life.*

The love, kindness, mercy, and salvation of God, the Father, came through Jesus. Everything in us that is well-pleasing in the sight of God, is through Him, even the gift of eternal life itself.

God saves His people to the hope of eternal life so it is not acquired by labor nor purchased but is a gift to His children. Those who have believed in God are under great obligations to perform good works for the love of Christ should compel them.

We are the only persons that can do them well. Through love, our good works are useful to influence our families and others to have faith, hope, love, and cheerful obedience to God.

ABBA Father, I make your Word the plan for my day. I focus on fulfilling your word over anything else and I will be led to your perfect will. Everything I see speaks to me of your great power. How magnificent Heaven must be. I celebrate your name as my Creator.

I need your potter's hands to mold me into the likeness of Christ. Refine me and make me willing to be all that you want me to be or as little as you want me to be. Help me to do good works that give you glory and are profitable to everyone around me.

Father, I need your help to follow the example of Jesus by showing kindness and love. Amen.

Faithful Promise

Romans 4:20-22: *Yet he did not waver through unbelief regarding the promise of God but was strengthened in his faith and gave glory to God, being fully persuaded that God had power to do what he had promised. This is why "it was credited to him as righteousness."*

1 Timothy 4:10: *That is why we labor and strive, because we have put our hope in the living God, who is the Savior of all people, and especially of those who believe.*

2 Peter 3:8-9: *But do not forget this one thing, dear friends: With the Lord a day is like a thousand years, and a thousand years are like a day. The Lord is not slow in keeping his promise, as some understand slowness. Instead he is patient with you, not wanting anyone to perish, but everyone to come to repentance.*

We can trust in the living God, for the accomplishment of His promises, who has power and therefore can and is faithful and will. For this reason, we have faith to trust in Him since He is the living God. He has life in Himself and is the author and giver of life, natural and spiritual. Those that believe in Christ are protected from many enemies and are delivered out of many afflictions and temptations. He is the Savior of all men: a great reason to trust in Him for the fulfillment of the promise of eternal life.

ABBA Father, the scriptures are filled with your promises for me. I take one today, hold to it, and live considering it.

Father, you dwell in me and walk with me. I confess my sins. You are faithful and just to forgive my sins and to cleanse me from all unrighteousness. Jesus has been made unto me wisdom, righteousness, sanctification, and redemption.

I pray today for more clarity and understanding of your Holy Word for myself and to share with others. Father, help me to meditate and pray your Word which is my living bread to sustain me daily. Amen.

Keep His Ways

Joshua 22:5 (MEV): *Only carefully obey the commandment and the law that Moses the servant of the Lord commanded you: to love the Lord your God, to walk in all His ways, to obey His commandments, to cling to Him, and to serve Him with all your heart and soul.*

Job 23:10-11: *But he knows the way that I take; when he has tested me, I will come forth as gold. My feet have closely followed his steps; I have kept to his way without turning aside.*

Psalm 37:34: *Hope in the Lord and keep his way. He will exalt you to inherit the land; when the wicked are destroyed, you will see it.*

Trust in the Word of the Lord for the manifestation of His promises, in which He never fails, and wait for deliverance out of every affliction. However, we must keep His Ways, which God has pointed out in His Word, and has directed His children to walk in.

Oftentimes, we will be tempted by the devil to turn aside to the right hand or the left and wicked men criticize and seek to pervert God's Word. Yet when we keep a tenacious study of the Word, then apply the Word to our lives, good comes of it in peace and the presence of God. Very soon we will dwell in the new Heaven and new earth with Christ and enjoy our eternal inheritance.

ABBA Father, I thank you for being my help and my deliverer. You are my strength in times of trouble and I put all my trust in you. I commit any sorrows, rejections, frustrations, or broken dreams into your hands. I believe you will bring me out.

The Word became flesh and dwelt among us. Jesus, you are the living bread that gives me life. Father, thank you for the spiritual bread from Heaven. Amen.

Uncertain Riches

Job 31:24 (ERV): *I have never trusted in riches. I never said even to pure gold, you are my hope.*

Psalm 52:7-8 (MEV): *"See, this is the man who did not make God his refuge, but trusted in the abundance of riches, and grew strong in his own wickedness." But I am like a green olive tree in the house of God; I trust in the mercy of God forever and ever.*

1 Timothy 6:17-19 (MEV): *Command those who are rich in this world that they not be conceited, nor trust in uncertain riches, but in the living God, who richly gives us all things to enjoy. Command that they do good, that they be rich in good works, generous, willing to share, and laying up in store for themselves a good foundation for the coming age, so that they may take hold of eternal life.*

In the Bible, Job purges himself from idolatry. When a selfish man is an idolater, he worships his gold and silver, putting his trust and confidence in them. However, to make gold the object of hope is to place it before God, whom every good man should trust and make his only hope. Therefore, not gold or riches, but Christ and His righteousness are the foundation of hope.

If in this life men only have hope in uncertain riches, they are miserable because trust in uncertain riches is unsatisfying. What is more satisfying is to put hope in the living God, who gives all things to enjoy and a future of His everlasting happiness.

Father, I praise you and bless you. Help me to be satisfied and not to be covetous. No matter what the circumstance, no matter what goes on around me or against me, I praise you. I praise you with joyful lips. I speak out in psalms, hymns, and make melody, with all my heart, to you. I am grateful for your blessings on this earth and my inheritance in Heaven. Amen.

Hope Is ... For You

Psalm 130:4-6 (AMPC): *But there is forgiveness with You [just what man needs], that You may be reverently feared and worshiped. I wait for the Lord, I expectantly wait, and in His word do I hope. I am looking and waiting for the Lord more than watchmen for the morning, I say, more than watchmen for the morning.*

Proverbs 10:28-29 (MEV): *The hope of the righteous will be gladness, but the expectation of the wicked will perish. The way of the Lord is strength to the upright, but destruction will come to the workers of iniquity.*

1 Corinthians 13:13 (AMPC): *And so faith, hope, love abide [faith—conviction and belief respecting man's relation to God and divine things; hope—joyful and confident expectation of eternal salvation; love—true affection for God and man, growing out of God's love for and in us], these three; but the greatest of these is love.*

The hope of the righteous is contentment. He can rejoice in the grace of hope as to future things. The expectation of his hope will be an entrance into the joy of the Lord and being brought into His presence.

The way of the Lord is strength to those who are upright in their heart. The Lord is their fortress and strong tower. While they are waiting and walking in the way of the Lord, He gives them courage and boldness so that they fear no enemy, nor any dangers and difficulties. But destruction will come to the workers of iniquity.

ABBA Father, I see all the sins and errors of my life as turning from curses to blessings. I thank you for the many blessings because I chose to obey your Word. I seek now to live a curse-free life, because of my cleansing.

Thank you, Father, that I eat the good of the land because you have given me a willing and obedient heart. Father, help me to have a deeper understanding of your Word and use wisdom to apply it to my life. Amen.

Believe In God's Promise

Joshua 21:44-45 (ERV): *And the Lord allowed them to have peace on all sides of their land, just as he had promised their ancestors. None of their enemies defeated them. The Lord allowed the Israelites to defeat every enemy. The Lord kept every promise that he made to the Israelites. There were no promises that he failed to keep. Every promise came true.*

Romans 4:18 (ERV): *There was no hope that Abraham would have children, but Abraham believed God and continued to hope. And that is why he became the father of many nations. As God told him, "You will have many descendants."*

Hebrews 10:23 (ERV): *We must hold on to the hope we have, never hesitating to tell people about it. We can trust God to do what he promised.*

Abraham believed and hoped in God's promise that he would become the father of many nations. He had been assisted by a supernatural aid in hope for the fulfillment of the promise by God's grace and power. Abraham believed against all visible and rational circumstances: Sarah's womb and his own body being old but God had said it. Therefore, like Abraham, our faith must rest upon the Word of God.

ABBA Father, thank you for your many blessings and promises. Father, you taught me to pray *Thy Kingdom come; Thy Will be done.* Today I recommit myself to you, my only Lord. Help me to join other members of your kingdom so that together we might become useful instruments in your hands.

Thank you for the promise through faith that one day I will be with you in Heaven. Amen.

Do You Need Hope?

Psalm 71:14 (CEV): I will never give up hope or stop praising you.

Lamentations 3:20-25 (NIRV): I remember it very well. My spirit is very sad deep down inside me. But here is something else I remember. And it gives me hope. The Lord loves us very much. So we haven't been completely destroyed. His loving concern never fails. His great love is new every morning. Lord, how faithful you are! I say to myself, "The Lord is everything I will ever need. So I will put my hope in him." The Lord is good to those who put their hope in him. He is good to those who look to him.

Romans 8:24-25 (CEB): We were saved in hope. If we see what we hope for, that isn't hope. Who hopes for what they already see? But if we hope for what we don't see, we wait for it with patience.

A believer must continually hope for deliverance and salvation from present troubles. The grace of hope is to be applied in times of affliction and distress. This grace is unique and powerful: it is an anchor to the soul when in distress, which keeps it firm and steadfast, and a helmet that covers the head on the day of battle.

The believer takes great pleasure in a perpetual grace and will praise the Lord for his renewed mercies. He is daily loaded with benefits.

ABBA Father, you are my only hope, in you I trust. My mouth is filled with praises because my help comes from you. Father, it's hard to imagine sometimes what it truly means to have your love.

Thank you for knowing how much I need you. I send you my love today. Amen.

Where Is Your Trust?

Psalm 62:7-8 (ERV): *My victory and honor come from God. He is the mighty Rock, where I am safe. People, always put your trust in God! Tell him all your problems. God is our place of safety. Selah.*

Proverbs 3:5-6 (ERV): *Trust the Lord completely, and don't depend on your own knowledge. With every step you take, think about what he wants, and he will help you go the right way.*

1 Timothy 6:17 (ERV): *Give this command to those who are rich with the things of this world. Tell them not to be proud. Tell them to hope in God, not their money. Money cannot be trusted, but God takes care of us richly. He gives us everything to enjoy.*

In this present world are those that are rich, dishonest, unsatisfied, and perishing. They that are high-minded with their wealth, look down from the height of their honor and riches with contempt upon the poor.

God chooses and calls the poor of this world for His purposes. Putting trust in uncertain riches is futile because they are here today and gone tomorrow. The providence of God is always best and safest in every circumstance and station of life to depend upon.

The living God, who is unchangeable, gives all things to enjoy. He should be trusted. Every good gift comes from God to enjoy and not to lay up or abuse, but to use for support and share with others.

ABBA Father, help me to only have unconditional love and obedience for you and your Word. Father, make my thoughts and plans agreeable to your will. Father, direct my steps to stand firmly and mature in spiritual growth. Father, help me to trust you and not have the love of money which is the root of all evil that leads to destruction. Amen.

Needs vs Wants

Psalm 23:1-3 (ERV): *The Lord is my shepherd. I will always have everything I need. He gives me green pastures to lie in. He leads me by calm pools of water. He restores my strength. He leads me on right paths to show that he is good.*

Proverbs 23:17-18 (ERV): *Never envy evil people, but always respect the Lord. This will give you something to hope for that will not disappoint you.*

Matthew 6:31-32 (ERV): *Don't worry and say, 'What will we eat?' or 'What will we drink?' or 'What will we wear?' That's what those people who don't know God are always thinking about. Don't worry because your Father in heaven knows that you need all these things.*

Many people are struggling these days in America, but many are also doing well. It is simply better not to look to others but look only to the Lord, pray, and patiently wait for His deliverance.

Don't let the success of others turn your head. Satan takes care of his own and his purpose is to promote love for the wrong things; things that God doesn't want in our lives.

America has long been a land where coveting has been a virtue, where we think we need things that we really don't. In the end, you only need God and, at the end of your life, if He is all you have then you have everything.

No wealthy or successful person who doesn't have Christ in their life has anything. Be thankful for Christ and His salvation and don't despair at what others have accomplished that you haven't. It's not about you, anyway, it's about Him. We are not saved by our own efforts but by Christ's.

Let Christ do for you, to you, and with you what His will is and be happy for your part in it. Quit struggling and trying to do things yourself. Don't envy others. Be faithful to God, He will lift you up.

ABBA Father, my need today is for my heart to obey your Word and my ears to receive your wisdom. I live my life today as an act of worship, a flowing of your love, and a dance of joy.

Father, thank you for sanctifying me by the Truth; Your Word is Truth. Amen.

God Is The Hope And Glory

Ephesians 1:11-14 (CEB): *We have also received an inheritance in Christ. We were destined by the plan of God, who accomplishes everything according to his design. We are called to be an honor to God's glory because we were the first to hope in Christ. You too heard the word of truth in Christ, which is the good news of your salvation. You were sealed with the promised Holy Spirit because you believed in Christ. The Holy Spirit is the down payment on our inheritance, which is applied toward our redemption as God's own people, resulting in the honor of God's glory.*

Colossians 1:26-27 (ERV): *This message is the secret truth that was hidden since the beginning of time. It was hidden from everyone for ages, but now it has been made known to God's holy people. God decided to let his people know just how rich and glorious that truth is. That secret truth, which is for all people, is that Christ lives in you, his people. He is our hope for glory.*

Titus 2:13 (ERV): *We should live like that while we are waiting for the coming of our great God and Savior Jesus Christ. He is our great hope, and he will come with glory.*

The Scriptures are a precious gift from God and written for our use and benefit. The Word of God is the greatest way to hope for which we must earnestly seek to study. Walking this Christian journey should not be just for our pleasure but for the glory of God and the good of others. The great end in all our actions must be that God may be glorified and we display love and kindness to those around us.

ABBA Father, I turn from all temptations, gods, idols, and sins. I see behind the temptation to the destruction that awaits. I love you with all my heart and thank you for the dreams that fill my heart.

Help me to be strong and wait patiently for the manifestation. Help me to be like-minded toward others according to Christ Jesus. Amen.

Confess Hope

Psalm 71:14-15 (CEV): *I will never give up hope or stop praising you. All day long I will tell the wonderful things you do to save your people. But you have done much more than I could possibly know.*

Romans 15:12-13 (CEV): *Isaiah says, "Someone from David's family will come to power. He will rule the nations, and they will put their hope in him." I pray that God, who gives hope, will bless you with complete happiness and peace because of your faith. And may the power of the Holy Spirit fill you with hope.*

Hebrews 10:23 (ERV): *We must hold on to the hope we have, never hesitating to tell people about it. We can trust God to do what he promised.*

Let us live by the confession of our faith and hope. In these scriptures, the writers refer to their reader's confession of hope in God. As a child of God and heir through faith in Christ, we have an assured right to hope for the Heavenly inheritance. All the promises of God will be made good to us if we stay committed to Him and His Word. Let us reflect on ways that we may influence and excite one another to love God, His people, all mankind, and to do good works.

Dear Jesus, I take upon myself your image. I confess the hope in the knowledge of the truth that you are sitting at our Father's right hand, interceding on my behalf.

Father, I thank you that my heart is good ground, that I hear and understand your Word. Your Word bears fruit in my life a hundredfold. I'm like a tree planted by the rivers of water that brings forth fruit in its season. My fruit will not wither and whatever I do will prosper. Amen.

God's Mercy

Deuteronomy 4:30-31: *When you are in distress and all these things have happened to you, then in later days you will return to the Lord your God and obey him. For the Lord, your God is a merciful God; he will not abandon or destroy you or forget the covenant with your ancestors, which he confirmed to them by oath.*

Lamentations 3:21-23 (MEV): *But this I call to mind, and therefore I have hope: It is of the Lord's mercies that we are not consumed; His compassions do not fail. They are new every morning; great is Your faithfulness.*

Hebrews 4:16: *Let us then approach God's throne of grace with confidence, so that we may receive mercy and find grace to help us in our time of need.*

God knows all the actions and desires of every person's heart. When we have God's favor towards us we need not fear whatever is against us. We can pray like the psalmist that the Lord's mercy is upon us to always have comfort according to the promise which is in His Word.

The Lord's watchful eye is over those who believe: hope is in His mercy. In difficulties and dangers, they will be helped and receive healing from any harm. Daily we have God's mercy for there is no running from Him, but by running toward Him we have hope.

ABBA Father, I consider how you have woven the threads of my life together for your good. Father, forgive me for the times I have walked around with a frown on my face. Remind me that everything around me brightens a little when I choose to smile. I am grateful that you are my hope. My heart rejoices because I can trust in your mercy every day. Amen.

Where Does Your Help Come From?

2 Chronicles 14:11 (KJ121): *And Asa cried unto the Lord his God and said, "Lord, it is nothing with Thee to help, whether with many or with those who have no power. Help us, O Lord our God, for we rest on Thee, and in Thy name we go against this multitude. O Lord, Thou art our God. Let not man prevail against Thee."*

Psalm 91:14-15 (ERV): *The Lord says, "If someone trusts me, I will save them. I will protect my followers who call to me for help. When my followers call to me, I will answer them. I will be with them when they are in trouble. I will rescue them and honor them.*

Isaiah 41:10-13: *So do not fear, for I am with you; do not be dismayed, for I am your God. I will strengthen you and help you; I will uphold you with my righteous right hand. All who rage against you will surely be ashamed and disgraced; those who oppose you will be as nothing and perish. Though you search for your enemies, you will not find them. Those who wage war against you will be as nothing at all. For I am the Lord your God who takes hold of your right hand and says to you, Do not fear; I will help you.*

The Bible gives us examples of those who have pleaded a case against their accusers who desired to hurt them. Many sought deliverance from all their troubles; that they should be healed of their sicknesses, both of soul and body. In Psalm 91, during his sufferings, the psalmist did not give up his hope in God. He believed that God would not only hear his cries during his pain, but hear the criticism of his enemies, and answer them at His appointed time.

DEVOTIONAL

ABBA Father, thank you for the gift of good health, peace, and life abundantly. Thank you for the gift of righteousness which I can do all things through Christ Jesus who strengthens me. Jesus is my light and I bring everything in my life unto Him. You know what I need to do and how I'll get there. Help me to take the most direct route to the things you want me to achieve by following You more closely. Amen.

Salvation Prayer

If you don't know Jesus as your Savior and Lord, open your heart and pray the following prayer in faith and Jesus will be your Lord!

ABBA Father, I come to you in the name of Jesus. Your Word says, *Whosoever shall call on the Name of the Lord shall be saved"* and *"If thou shalt confess with thy mouth the Lord Jesus, and shalt believe in thine heart that God hath raised Him from the dead, thou shalt be saved* (Acts 2:21; Romans 10:9). You said my salvation would be the result of your Holy Spirit giving me new birth by coming to live in me (John 3:5-6, 15-16; Romans 8:9-11) and that if I would ask, You would fill me with Your Holy Spirit and give me the ability to speak with other tongues (Luke 11:13; Acts 2:4). I believe it and Lord I receive it now.

I take you at Your Word. I confess with my mouth that Jesus Christ is Lord. And I believe in my heart that You raised Him from the dead. Thank You for coming into my heart, for giving me Your Holy Spirit as You have promised, and for being Lord over my life. Glory! Hallelujah!

Jesus, I bow down before Your throne of Grace and Mercy. I bless Your Holy Name. As my Alpha and Omega, my Beginning and my Ending I surrender my praise to You and You alone my Loving King of Kings. You are the Roaring Lion of Judah, all Powerful and Mighty and none can defy You. Knowing this I do rest assure that I am fully protected and saved. Mighty I stand! Allow me to blossom and emerge mighty; standing strong; ready to win any battle thrown my way all the days of my life That You may say well done. Grant me the strength to carry on and to move forward into victory. May I walk on the raging waters and dance in the pouring rain, for the battle is already won and I shall overcome. Amen!

Prayer To Mend Which Is Broken

ABBA Father, I call on you right now in a special way. It is through your power that I was created. Every breath I take, every morning I wake, and every moment of every hour, I live under your power.

ABBA Father, I ask you now to touch me with that same power. For if you created me from nothing, you can certainly recreate me for something. Fill me with the healing power of your Spirit. Blot out all my sins and iniquities. Cast out anything that should not be in me, especially those evil thoughts and wicked imaginations.

Mend what is broken. Root out any unproductive cells. Open any blocked arteries or veins and rebuild any damaged areas. Remove all inflammation in my infrastructure and cleanse any infection. Let the warmth of your healing love pass through my body to make new any unhealthy areas so that my body will function the way you created it to function.

And, ABBA Father, guide my feet upon the right pathways of holy living. Restore me to full health in mind and body so that I may serve you the rest of my life. I ask this through Jesus Christ our Lord. Amen.

DEVOTIONAL

About the Author

Evangelist Bridgette Michele Alfred has been married to Elder Tyrone Alfred for 30 years. She is the mother of four children (three daughters and one son: Cheraun, Tiffany, Tylisa, and Teon); the grandmother of four (three grandsons and one granddaughter: Deja, Dane, Dean and Jaden); one son-in-law, Kelvin, and one daughter-in-law, Valerie. Evangelist Alfred has an extended family with Alonzo, Timothy, Edna, and Cindy Campbell and their families.

Evangelist Bridgette was raised in Washington, D.C. She completed one year at the University of the District of Columbia majoring in Business Management. She is a Desert Storm Vet and served in the U.S. Army for 15 years. She retired in 2014 from the United States Capitol Police where she served for 24 years.

Evangelist Bridgette accepted Jesus Christ as her Lord and Savior at the age of 14 and received the baptism of the Holy Spirit with evidence of speaking in tongues in her early twenties.

After reading *The Purpose Driven Life* by Rick Warren in 2004, she asked ABBA Father to show her His purpose for her life. ABBA Father told Evangelist Bridgette to open a transitional home for women and children in crisis. Also, during this time, ABBA Father started dictating the musical *Jesus Saves the Hood* to her. ABBA Father's specific instructions were that this musical was a ministry for the lost, the hopeless, and the unsaved. ABBA Father is still strategically working out the details for the transitional home and the musical to come to fruition.

When There Is Hope (Healing Over Past Events) is the first published book written by Evangelist Bridgette. She is currently writing for an online magazine, *Urban Sentinel*, a daily Facebook page, *Hope Is Real Devotional*, and has plans for writing five more books.

Bibliography

Alfred, Bridgette M. *When There Is HOPE (Healing Over Past Events)*. Florida: Xulon Press Elite, 2018.

www.ingramcontent.com/pod-product-compliance
Lightning Source LLC
Chambersburg PA
CBHW071428070526
44578CB00001B/29